LETTERS OF A
PORTUGUESE NUN

MYRIAM CYR

LETTERS OF A PORTUGUESE NUN

*Uncovering the Mystery Behind
a Seventeenth-Century Forbidden Love*

A HISTORICAL MYSTERY

miramax books

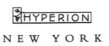

NEW YORK

ISBN 0-7868-6911-9

First Edition
10 9 8 7 6 5 4 3 2 1

For Gifford

CONTENTS

There will always be those who frown on forbidden love. But love, you see, does not care, for it, unlike prejudice, knows no boundaries.

A NOTE FROM THE AUTHOR

FIRST STUMBLED ACROSS THE LETTERS OF A POR-
tuguese nun in Montreal, at the Théâtre de
Quat' Sous (Four Penny Theater). The letters
were spoken in French in the form of a play,
and I was so moved that I immediately determined to
translate them. I was living in London at the time, performing for the Royal National Theater, and so I spent the
following six months using every spare minute I had in the
company of a dictionary and Mariana's words. Luckily for
me, I had no idea how famous the letters were, that some of
the greatest French actresses have performed them, or that
over the years they have been translated countless times in
several languages including English. Had I known, I proba-

bly never would have ventured into what would become an important journey of the heart.

I enlisted the wonderful director Lisa Forrell to direct a reading of the letters that took us first to a tiny theater above a pub in London and then to the Culture Project in New York. A book editor, also moved by the letters, approached me asking if I would consider writing Mariana's story, but I hesitated, having never written a book.

One stormy evening, the theater was empty except for a handful of people. At the end, I told what little I knew of Mariana's story. That she had existed, but that in recent years people mostly believed a man had written the letters. That night, a young seamstress from Brooklyn who had ventured out in this appalling weather came to me after the performance, in tears. She was going through a painful breakup and Mariana's letters had given her the words to describe everything she felt but had not been able to express until now. She was outraged at the thought that people would even consider that the letters might not be from Mariana, and I thought of the times when, as women, we are not heard and how after 300 years, Mariana, whose words have changed so many lives, is not allowed the most basic of rights, to claim her own voice.

This book is for my friend Lisa Forrell, for the seamstress from Brooklyn, whose name I do not know, but most of all, for Mariana. I had no idea she would lead me into a world more dangerous, more magical, and more intriguing than I could ever have imagined.

In the three years it has taken me to research this book, I was struck by the unreliability of historical accounts. The telling of events varied greatly depending on the source, and in some instances, a same event was described as having taken place in different years altogether, sometimes involving a protagonist of the opposite gender. Taking this into account, I decided to always read a minimum of three or four renditions of specific events in the hope of piecing together a somewhat accurate picture of what had occurred. Original documents were consulted whenever possible. Dates and the spelling of names of that time period are often inconsistent, first names are seldom quoted, and so I have provided the modern English versions of the names whenever available.

There exists an old Portuguese custom that was prevalent in Mariana's day. If a man stared intently into a woman's eyes, it meant he wanted her to become his lover. If the woman returned the gaze, her answer was yes.

This book is a work of nonfiction but before the prologue begins and the facts take over, please allow me a brief flight of fancy.

As Mariana says in one of her letters: "I could not stop myself from telling you this as well."

PORTUGAL 1667

THE OFFICERS RODE UP ALONGSIDE THE CONVENT WALL, gesturing as they passed by, anxious to get to their lodgings. The men were excited. This was their last trip back to Beja before the next battle.

The nun had not seen the French officer for some time, and she was impatient for his return. He halted a short distance from the wall, steadying his mount before gazing up toward her with a silent fixed stare. That afternoon, in the white winter sun of Portugal, she was forced to equate the sharpening of her senses to the feelings called up by the man sitting motionless before her. Until this moment, she had refused to name what she felt, but the mixture of dread and joy was so overwhelming, the surge that flooded her entire body so immeasurable, she could do nothing but acknowledge her feelings. She stared back. She forgot her surroundings and the impossibility of what lay before her. She experienced certainty, when in the briefest of moments, everything changes.

And then he was off, and the moment was gone. She placed a hand on the thick parapet wall. She owed much to her vocation. When they had cut her hair, she had not seen it as an imposition so much as a necessity, brought on by her gender and war. It had seemed a small price to pay in comparison to all she gained.

She remembered how one day, not so long ago, her brother, returning from battle, had brought back a Spanish sword for her to see. Its uniqueness lay in the blade, finely sharpened on all sides. She had admired its precision. Her brother had let her hold it. The blade gave its owner a feeling of strength and power, but also that of emptiness and finality. The inevitability of it had made her sway slightly.

Facing the expanse before her, she faltered again. For the first time, she recognized the meaning of the black veil that fell beyond her shoulders. Freedom without freedom. Love without love. Like the Spanish sword, she saw that the life she had come to cherish would, from now on, be double-edged.

PROLOGUE

HEN, IN 1669, A FAMOUS PARISIAN BOOKSELLER published a slim volume called *Portuguese Letters*, the title referred to a collection of five illicit love letters written by a nun to a French officer. Their love had flourished a few years earlier, during Portugal's struggle for independence. The bookseller, chancing upon the letters, sensed a potential windfall and brought them to press while the officer in question was away, fighting a new war.

The letters took Paris by storm. The nun spoke of love in a manner so direct, so precise and so familiar, she sent shivers of recognition through the sophisticated strata of polite society. Copies flew off the shelves. Weeks later, counterfeit editions were in circulation. The book, small enough to be concealed by a fan, shed a light of self-awareness over the dissipation of the *grand siècle* and threatened to upset the delicate balance of power between men and women.

The officer returned to find young, nubile, aristocratic women swooning in his presence. The name of the nun, however, remained unknown, and a growing undercurrent questioned the authenticity of the letters. The officer neither denied, nor confirmed the affair. Within months, a campaign was afoot discrediting the possibility that a nun could have written such passionate letters.

Not until 1810, close to a hundred and fifty years later, did a monk, who belonged to the same religious order as the nun, step forward to reveal her name. The erudite Franciscan scholar, Jean-François Boissonade, already famous for championing the Greek poetess Sappho, published a small article under the pseudonym Omega in the *Journal de l'Empire:*

Everyone knows today that these Letters, filled with intelligence and passion were written to M. de Chamilly by a Portuguese nun and that the translation is by Guilleragues or Subligny. But bibliographers have not yet discovered the name of the nun. I may inform them. On my copy of the edition of the Portuguese Letters there is a note written by a hand that is to me unknown: "the nun who wrote these letters was named Mariana Alcoforada,[1] nun in Beja, between l'Estremadura and Andalusia. The chevalier to whom they were written was the Count of Chamilly, then named the Count of

Saint-Léger." [. . .] One hundred and forty years have gone by since the *Lettres Portugaises* were written and make my indiscretion forgivable. Such an old story can no longer feed malicious gossip or spite.[2]

Diligent efforts from Portuguese historians unearthed documents proving Mariana's existence. Scholars and artists rose in her defense. Modigliani, Matisse, and Braque tried to imagine her. Rilke and Stendhal championed her, and it has been suggested that Elizabeth Barrett Browning's acclaimed *Sonnets from the Portuguese* owe much of their inspiration to the letters.

Yet to this day, controversy still rages. A plethora of books and scholarly essays conclude the impossibility of female authorship. These scholars argue that the letters are, in fact, a fabrication written on a dare by a French aristocrat, who was famous among his friends for creating a romantic, rhyming game called "Valentines."

The main proponents of this theory, French scholars Jacques Rougeot and Frédéric Deloffre, dismiss the possibility that Mariana was capable of writing the letters: "Admit that the *Portuguese Letters* were written in a convent, by a nun with little if any instruction, having never known the world, is to believe that spontaneity and pure passion inspired a woman to write a superior work of art over and above what the best minds of the greatest period of French literature could offer their public."[3]

History speaks differently. Tucked away in the confines of

Portugal, Mariana Alcoforado was twenty-six years old. She was a scribe, and as such, she held one of the highest and most respected positions in the convent. Her country was at war with Spain and these troubled times granted her more freedom than most women of her day. There was only one dominion she was not allowed to conquer; she could never know secular love. Yet through her comes one of the most exquisite treasures of universal literature. Five letters, written over a few months, that chart unrequited love in ways so tender and exacting that three hundred years later, they haunt us still.

As remarkable as the letters are themselves, they are rivaled by the story that surrounds them. The officer and the nun met at a time when the music of Purcell graced the court of England. In Amsterdam, Vermeer was about to paint one of his most famous portraits, *Girl with a Pearl Earring,* and in France, King Louis XIV was entering the greatest years of his reign, throwing lavish parties and commissioning ballets meant for him to dance. Mariana's time was one of excesses, and the whims of politics and the ambitions of Royals would preside over her fate.

While scholars now acknowledge that Mariana existed, most do not accept her as the author of the letters, preferring to believe they were written by a man.

There is a medieval scientific principal called Occam's razor that states that the simplest answer is most likely the true one.

Here are the circumstances surrounding the affair.

1

MARIANA'S WORLD

"Because we men cannot resist temptation, is that a reason women ought not, when the whole of their education is caution and warning against our attempts? Do not their grandmothers give them one easy rule? Men are to ask, women are to deny."

SAMUEL RICHARDSON, *Clarissa*, 1748
(inspired by the Portuguese letters)

"Were men capable of reason in their choices they should attach themselves to nuns rather than to other women. Nothing prevents nuns from reflecting incessantly on their passion, they are not distracted by a thousand things that dissipate and occupy the world."

MARIANA ALCOFORADO, LETTER 5

ONG BEFORE ENGLAND TOOK TO THE SEAS TO BUILD its empire, the tiny country of Portugal ruled the oceans, making it one of the most powerful nations of the Western Hemisphere.

During the fifteenth and sixteenth centuries, Portugal, roughly the size of the state of Maine, dominated world trade. Its dominion extended to India, Africa, Asia, and South America. Goods flowed into Portugal from distant, inaccessible lands. The Portuguese wrote letters on scented paper drenched in saffron. Quills were dipped in ink found in remote Chinese provinces and featured feathers plucked from exotic African birds. Persian rugs purchased with South American silver hung on Portuguese walls. Gold flowed in from Asia and Africa. The Portuguese built

Macao and passed the South African Cape of Good Hope before Christopher Columbus. Portugal was the first to establish trading posts in Japan. The Portuguese nation presided over the Turks, the Arabs, the Moors, and at its height, Portugal's empire was greater than that of the Romans.[1]

By the beginning of the seventeenth century, however, Portugal was spiraling downward. Spain, crossing the border, had usurped the Portuguese crown and imposed its rule. Sixty years of abusive leadership had reduced these once proud people to a chaotic collection of individuals at a loss for a sense of purpose. Universal poverty plagued the population. Disregarding laws, bands of monks flooded city streets at sundown to commit murders that went unpunished.[2] Highway robbers ruled the countryside, making travel unsafe. Men paraded multiple swords at their sides. Pistols, daggers, and illegal knives with diamond tips were worn as much for show as for protection. Bullfights were the nation's favorite pastime. Licentiousness was rampant. Illegitimate children were so common among the clergy, it was not unusual for priests to seek favors from government officials to help place their sons or marry off their daughters. Men wasted away their days by playing cards, dice, palm games, skittles, lawn bowling, chess, checkers, and ball games. Fidalgos, the title given to nobility, bickered amongst themselves over promotions that meant nothing. The few patricians who retained some sense of pride were pushed aside in favor of groveling upstarts.

Discontent reached new heights the day Spain, endlessly at war with the rest of Europe, started sending young Portuguese noblemen to die in Spanish wars. The unwarranted loss of life, coupled with a sudden increase in Spanish taxes, finally compelled the Fidalgos into action. Portugal rose against Spain in December 1640. On a dewy Saturday morning, the royal ancestral house of Braganza engaged in a war of independence that would last twenty-eight years.[3]

A FEW MONTHS EARLIER, ON APRIL TWENTY-SECOND, UNNOTICED, the christening of Mariana Alcoforado took place in the beautiful white chapel of Santa-Maria situated a few feet from her parents' home. Christenings usually occurred quickly following the birth of a child because of high infant mortality, and it is safe to assume that Mariana was born during the week preceding the ceremony.

The chapel of Santa-Maria belonged to the picturesque town of Beja situated in the lower Alentejo, Portugal's most southern province.[4] An important agricultural center, flourishing principally on the trade of wheat and olive oil, Beja counted 3,000 residents, twenty-six churches, and seven religious institutions. Built on a hill, surrounded by olive groves, the town overlooked vast and solitary plains. Little red windmills, used to grind endless fields of wheat, punctuated an otherwise empty horizon. Because of its proximity to the Spanish border, Beja was the ideal garrison town, and Mariana would grow up surrounded by foreigners.

Mariana was the second of five daughters and three sons born to Francisco da Costa Alcoforado and Leonor Mendes. Francisco's firstborn, Ana, was destined to marry while Mariana and her sisters would enter convent life. Ana's fate was more precarious than Mariana's. Once married, Ana would be treated no better than a slave.[5]

Portuguese Catholicism, a mixture of leftover Muslim customs, pagan beliefs, and religious devotions, was the ideal arena in which to subjugate women. Wives were deliberately kept illiterate. They wore a Catholic version of the chador in the shape of a veil that hung over their faces. They ate on the floor, sitting on mats made out of cork, while men sat at tables. Husbands barred the windows and bolted the doors of their homes. Women were forbidden from walking in streets unless they were accompanied either by their husbands, a family member, or a retinue of servants.

Men looked down on women traveling alone and pinched the calves and arms of any woman traveling by herself, often leaving the unfortunate victim severely bruised. The practice was so frequent that the Spanish had dubbed the behavior a *Portuguese kindness*.[6] Royal edicts further sought to control women. Women found conversing on church steps were threatened with prison and deportation.[7]

These laws attempted rather unsuccessfully to curb women and men's behavior resulting from the Portuguese passion for love. Love was at the epicenter of seventeenth-century Portuguese life. Peasant women embroidered the word *amor* (love) on their purses, and a woman, regardless of her rank, marital status, place and time of day, stared fixedly at the man she liked to let him know he could declare himself without hesitation. A chronicler of the period, Mme. de Ratazzi, in her book *Le Portugal à vol d'oiseau (A Bird's Eye View of Portugal)*, comments that love held such an important place in everyday life that there was little room for anything else. All conversations revolved around and had to do with love. Men, whether old, young, ugly, handsome, uneducated, scholarly, civil, or military spoke only of their female conquests. Removed from political or administrative powers by the Spanish, the Portuguese male kept busy standing below balconies serenading loved ones.

Locked-up wives found ways to take on lovers. Men used love to indulge in fights, skirmishes, and heated exchanges. Honor and pride fueled jealous behavior. Illegal duels were hailed as acts of courage, and dying of love was considered the most noble of deeds.

Nuns were not excluded from the frenzy. So many men fell in love with nuns, they became known as *freiráticos* (nun lovers). These spiritual and platonic relationships were considered the highest and most worthy form of love. Men failed to see the irony inherent in keeping their wives uneducated and sequestered, while, at the same time, seeking out erudite nuns over whom they had no power. Though convents served as refuges for women seeking protection from the vagaries of war, finance was generally the greatest motivator sending daughters to a nunnery. Francisco's decision to marry off his eldest daughter, Ana, and relegate Mariana and her sisters to a convent had primarily to do with protecting his hard-won assets.

Mariana's father came from the harsh and unrelenting climate of northern Portugal beyond the mountains that divide the country. The Alcoforados were impoverished gentry and ambition pushed Francisco south to the warmer, more indulgent Alentejo, in search of opportunity. With little to offer except his name, Francisco married the daughter of a wealthy merchant. Not much is known about Mariana's mother, but according to her will, Leonor Mendes' marriage to Francisco was one of respect. She kept most of her wealth and was able to bequeath goods to her children. A shrewd businessman, Francisco prospered and by the time Mariana was eight years old, he had become an influential man with connections to the king and high-ranking officials. An elected alderman of the city of Beja, a court administrator, assessor, and tax collector, Francisco was also responsible for the transportation of wheat and the processing of flour. He managed a stud farm, had recently been appointed judge, and to his great pride, he had been awarded the mantle of Knight of the Order of Christ.[8]

Francisco fathered a son before marrying, but this did not hinder his reputation. Francisco placed this son, José, in the priesthood, and the relationship must have been cordial because José christened the last of Francisco's eight legitimate children.

To prevent his land from being fragmented at his death, Francisco married off Ana, his eldest, and willed the entirety of his assets to his firstborn legal heir, Balthazar, born five years after Mariana. He placed his remaining daughters into a convent, and destined his other sons for religious or military service. A common practice, this prevented estates from being divided between offspring, but Francisco was so intent in protecting the family name he added strange clauses to his testament dated September 30, 1660; the heir would lose his succession rights if he failed to abide by any one of them.

- The heir was responsible for increasing the estate a third of its third.
- If the successor ended up being a woman, the husband was obliged to keep and carry the Alcoforado surname.
- Should any beneficiary commit a crime of lese majesty (any offense against God, king, or honor) or any other crime that involved the confiscation of wealth, the inheritance would be revoked retroactively, two hours before the crime was committed.

■ Nuns and priests were not able to inherit, unless there were no other living secular children.

His last wish was to be lowered in the ground, dressed and armed in his Knights of Christ clothing, wearing a red cap, swords at his flank, and high-laced boots and spurs.

Francisco did everything to insure the Alcoforado name would survive him. He instilled a deep sense of pride for the family name in all his children. Education and social standing were clearly important to him and he took the unusual step of seeing to the education of all his sons and daughters. He kept books in his house. His friends included the Portuguese ambassador to France. A fierce patriot, Francisco insisted his sons become expert horsemen, ready to defend their country.

Raised amidst politics and patriotism, Mariana spent her time between the manor house in the city and her father's immense rural estate. Large open spaces reaching into infinity colored her days. Children were left to their own devices, and she and her siblings ran alongside the myriad of servants that populated the households, darting around huge silos used to store the wheat her father grew. Francisco's stud farm was extremely lucrative. Horses were rare in Portugal since mules were the preferred mode of transport, and Mariana's father benefited from hefty royal subsidies for housing horses between military campaigns.

For reasons unknown, Mariana's time with her family

was abruptly interrupted at the age of ten when her father placed her in a convent before she was legally of age. A papal bull, waiving the age limit, was normally required for girls entering religious life before the age of twelve, but since the beginning of war all ties with Rome were severed at the behest of Spain, making the paperwork impossible to obtain. The decision therefore lay with the abbess. The old and wise Madre Maria de Mendonca must have appreciated the advantages of acquiring an Alcoforado girl and knew better than to let such an opportunity slip by. Mariana was not quite eleven when she officially began her novitiate.

Francisco chose the best and most prestigious religious institution of the city. Up Beja's narrow, roughly cobbled streets, adjacent to the town's castle, stood the convent of Our Lady of Concieção, arguably the finest in Portugal.[9] Founded in 1467 by Dom Fernando and Dona Beatriz, the parents of King Dom Manuel, the convent was favored by royal and private donations, making it one of the wealthiest institutions of its kind.

The convent of Concieção was built at the very southern edge of town, a street away from the Alcoforado household. A dazzling, intricately sculpted stone frieze surrounded the white convent walls, accentuating the beauty and sophisticated simplicity of the architecture. Inside, delicate hand-painted blue and white tiles underlined beautiful tinted windows, markers of a Moorish occupation. The chapter-house where the nuns came to deliberate would soon be reconstructed, and the chapels sheltered gilded altars and ornately sculpted pews. The walls and ceilings were covered with decorative arabesques and stunning frescoes of Arab inspiration that were elegant and deeply feminine.

Mariana's contract was signed on a Monday, January 2, 1651. Men and ladies of importance always traveled with a retinue of servants and clerks, and Mariana most probably reached the convent carried on a donkey's back. A second donkey transported the sack of gold coins needed to buy Mariana her entrance to the convent, and a third would have balanced a small wooden chest that held her few worldly possessions. Her father, no doubt dressed in his judicial robes, led the procession. Her family house faced one of the convent walls, and she had only to turn a street corner to reach the hundred steps that led to the imposing arched convent doors. Though young, the significance of the event cannot have escaped her. From this day onward, she would abandon the outside world, never to leave the confines of the convent for as long as she would live.

The papers describing the event indicate that Mariana's father drove a hard bargain in favor of his daughter. Francisco's terms stipulated that Mariana retain her name in spite of the customary religious renaming and that the convent renounce all claims to her inheritance. In return, Mariana's father handed over three hundred thousand reis. Sixty-two and a half gold coins were quickly counted and whisked away to be safely stored in the convent vault. Roughly equivalent to thirteen thousand U.S. dollars, this was a sizable sum for the time. An additional amount would be paid once Mariana took her vows at sixteen, and Francisco's estate agreed to furnish the convent with a barrel of wheat each August for the next one hundred and fifty years.

Mariana's father requested that a private dwelling be built for his daughter. Called *sua casas* (their houses) by the nuns, these were freestanding structures intended to keep the wealthy and well-born separated from the less fortunate. These houses, strictly forbidden by the Convent Rule, nevertheless existed. Mariana's house would have two rooms with windows, one to sleep in and the other to live in. The houses sometimes had two doors but they were always built in such a way that the abbess could lock them at night. Francisco would also contribute toward building a new dormitory for the overpopulated convent and as more of his daughters entered religious life, he would build more houses for them.

The convent relied on government stock, rents, state pensions, church offerings, and nuns' dowries for income, and Mariana's hefty contribution was well received. It would be invested and the resulting interest would become Mariana's rent and go toward maintaining the convent.

Admittance criteria stipulated that a girl entering the convent of Concieção must be from a good and virtuous family. She must be free of any contagious disease, prepared to carry on religious work, possess a courageous disposition, and be at least twelve years of age. Mariana would turn eleven in April.

The law required Mariana to be present at the signing of the contract. Made to wait in an antechamber while her father negotiated, she was called in before witnesses at the end of the meeting. The same law also requested that the Convent Rule be read aloud to her, thereby insuring she entered religious life of her own free will.

- ■ A nun must participate in all choir duties and in the execution of divine rites. Should a nun shirk her religious duties, she would have to declare her fault publicly in the refectory. A second infraction would entail rations of bread and water. A third would trigger corporal discipline. Should these measures fail, her veil would be removed, and the offending nun would not be allowed to approach the altar (unable to practice her religious faith in the house of God), the parlor (unable to see visitors), the service entrances (prohibiting the nun from the only physical contact she could have with the outside world), or the kitchens (where scraps of delicious pastries were sometimes handed out), until she changed her ways.
- ■ Silence must be observed from the first call to bed until the first call to rise, and utmost efforts would be made to maintain silence during the day.

■ Nuns must abstain from private friendships and/or physical contact with one another, under penalty of losing their voting rights for two years. (Major decisions concerning the community were taken by vote, from the choice of the abbess, who was elected every three years, to extra holidays, and voting rights were considered extremely important.) If these actions did not deter the offending nuns, subsequent transgressions would result in placing them in a correction home for a period of four months.

■ An abbess guilty of condoning such infractions would be suspended from her office duties for a period of three months, would not be allowed to write letters, receive visits, or engage in rapports that included lengthy conversations, writing, sending and receiving gifts.

■ Religious habits must be modest. They must not be allowed to drag and could not serve to hide high-heeled shoes, full or wide skirts, or dresses as often was the case. A nun whose appearance would be deemed inappropriate or immodest would not be allowed access to the parlor.

■ If a nun left the cloister, she would be excommunicated. The excommunication could only be reversed in an open community vote and only if the nun was able to prove that she had not communicated with anyone while she was outside convent walls.

■   If a nun was found alone with a man, in or out of the convent, even if the man was a church official, the nun would be condemned to ten years of solitary confinement and incarcerated in the rat-infested underground prison situated on the convent premises, and forever deprived of attending religious occasions, approaching the convent's gates or the service entrances.

Whether or not Mariana agreed with the Convent Rule was not really a concern. The reality was that Mariana, the child, had no say in the matter. Her eyes resolutely kept toward the floor, simply nodding her head in sign of acceptance, Mariana showed no emotion; faced with adversity, Portuguese aristocracy never did.[10]

DESPITE THE APPARENT SEVERITY, MARIANA SOON DISCOVERED that life at Concieção operated under different rules than those read out loud to her. Unlike her sister Ana who was about to marry a man twice her age, here at Concieção Mariana would be mistress of her fate. Nuns would teach her how to read and write. In times of famine, she would be among the last to go hungry, and her religious status would grant her the right to speak to men as an equal.

Mariana belonged to the Franciscan order of the Poor Ladies of Clare established in 1212. Clare was a saintly woman whose reputation for holiness had prompted

Saint Francis of Assisi to invite her to join him in making vows of poverty in imitation of Christ. Encouraged by Saint Francis, Clare founded a female version of his order and took to the streets, freely performing good works. Within four years, her apostolate had become so powerful that the Pope, fearful of the respect she and her order commanded, forced the Poor Ladies of Clare into cloisters. Over the next centuries, the nuns were obligated to break their vows of poverty and accept land and possessions.

Subsequent dire economic straits slowly transformed Clare's original intent, and the nuns eventually opened their doors to benefactors who could provide them with sustenance. In return, the benefactors expected to be entertained, and the religious parlors became available to men at any hour of the days or nights. Men supplied the nuns with money, goods, and favors in exchange for time spent in their company. The nuns became practiced musicians, versed in politics, science, and the arts, providing the men with a soothing refuge from the vicissitudes of life. Over time, protected by influential patrons, the nuns transformed their cloisters into powerful institutions.

Lax morals peaked by the mid-sixteenth century and a Spanish nun, Saint Teresa of Ávila, appalled by the rampant materialism and lack of spiritual values she found in convents, instigated a vast religious reform.[11] By the time Mariana came to live at Conciação, Saint Teresa's new moral code was sweeping through European convents. Portuguese nuns, however, ignored Saint Teresa's apostolate because Spain, the mightiest Catholic power in Christendom, had forced Rome to interrupt all diplomatic relations with Portugal. With no bishops to enforce religious law, abbesses were free to conduct religious business as they saw fit, and the Portuguese convents flourished under the governance of educated women.

Beauty and purposefulness greeted visitors when entering the convent of Conciecão. Described as a paradise of fragrant flowers, the city location did not allow for vegetable gardens or orchards, but there were no fences either. Instead, vast terraces and balconies allowed the nuns to see beyond the tall walls onto the vast and beautiful Alentejo plains. The convent housed several varieties of trees that produced luscious oranges, almonds, and olives. A beautiful drinking well, from which the nuns drew water throughout the day, adorned an inner courtyard surrounded by stone archways lined with marble benches and sculpted basins.

Much of the convent food came from farms and dairies the convent owned and administered. The rest of the goods, like salt and sugar, were bought at markets or wholesale. Goods were bartered or obtained by way of petitions made directly to the king. Because nuns were held in high regard, they negotiated the most advantageous prices from local merchants and even from abroad. Cloth, needles, and thread came from France or England. The nuns purchased fabric from the best millineries in Europe.

A city within a city, Mariana's convent lodged two hundred and fifty nuns, thirty-eight novices, and eighteen students, of which Mariana was one. Abandoned noblewomen and the poor were given shelter. One hundred and forty-nine servants and maids catered to the nuns' every need. Priests lived on the premises. The nuns employed general prosecutors, a judge, and a clerk. The convent operated its own apothecary, staffed a doctor, a surgeon, and a man to administer bloodlettings, the popular treatment for many ills. There was a butler, two chapel stewards, a candle maker, a soap maker, two messengers, and one mule driver. There was a dedicated area for the killing of animals, another to prepare the meat. Carpenters, masons, shepherds (they owned four hundred sheep), eighty-seven day laborers, one wine cellar attendant, monks, and hospice employees were all part of a population of seven hundred and six.

Madre Maria de Mendonca, the abbess who had negotiated Mariana's dowry, tutored the young Mariana personally. Under her loving care and the expert guidance of the nuns, Mariana became versed in Latin, Spanish, French,[12] mathematics, music, history, geography, and science. The convent owned fifty-one books, an impressive number for the time. Between lessons and religious duties, Mariana led a worldly existence. Servants attended to her needs, communicating with the outside world, transporting letters, collecting news and goods. For Mariana, who was rich and the daughter of one of Beja's most influential citizens, the Convent Rule applied, more or less.

The young novitiates learned the art of serving tea and how to make the delicious pastries Portuguese convents were so famous for. The Concieção pastries were reputed the best in Portugal. Mariana was probably taught to play a string or wind instrument and perhaps even how to dance. A French dignitary visiting a convent in the Azores a few years after Mariana's story speaks of being treated to a wonderful entertainment where nuns danced exquisitely and the priest excelled at the fandango.

Mariana grew amidst erudite and often beautiful women who brought art and expertise to the entertaining of men. Portuguese aristocrats, wealthy merchants, and university students spent most of their free time in their company. Problems arose when *freiráticos* found themselves more passionate than reasonable. Convents struggled to maintain the delicate balance between encouraging possible benefactors while at the same time discouraging the men from aspiring to a more physical form of love.

Two years after Mariana entered the convent, the king, concerned by the growing cases of men falling in love with nuns, issued an edict:

Further to penalties already in place, considering the abuse that many lay persons commit by frequenting assiduously certain convent gates, all persons proven to frequent nuns' convents will be punishable of two months of prison and will not be released before having paid eighty thousand reis (two thousand U.S. dollars) in fines that will be used to cover war expenses.

[King John VI, 1653]

This law, however, and others like it, had little effect.

The seasons passed. At sixteen, Mariana's hair was cut short as a sign of abnegation, and the young Alcoforado girl formally entered the community. The nuns had produced a young woman sure of herself and of her station in life and ready to meet the world. Mariana's faith must have resembled that of the women around her, unquestioned but colored with pragmatism. The long black shroud that replaced her white veil was perhaps more symbolic of taking on a profession, than answering a calling.

The year after Mariana took her vows, the convent began renovations on the chapterhouse. Artisans, painters, and day laborers must have created a welcome commotion, brightening the walls with fresh paint and making the chapterhouse one of the nicest and most feminine in Portugal, but the realities of war were quick to reassert themselves. Famine struck in 1659, and the convent found itself in dire straits. That year, with one hundred and eighty-five contracts outstanding, the nuns owed money to farmers, laborers, and purveyors of goods. A younger sister, Catarina, joined Mariana some time during this period. Probably a sickly child, Catarina died before Mariana reached her twentieth birthday: there is no mention of her beyond 1660.

2

WAR, POLITICS, AND THE FRENCH

"Diligence and expeditiousness are of all military virtues, those who, the most, contribute to success, but only when they are accompanied by prudence and circumspection."

HENRI DE LA TOUR-D'AUVERGNE,
VISCOUNT OF TURENNE (1611–1675), FRENCH COMMANDER-IN-CHIEF,
OVERSEEING THE PORTUGUESE WAR UNDER LOUIS XIV

"You were obliged to go and serve your king; if all that is said of him is true, he does not need your help and he would have excused you."

MARIANA ALCOFORADO, LETTER 2

Y THE TIME MARIANA TURNED TWENTY-TWO YEARS old, Portugal's armed forces were depleted and its coffers were empty. Numbers of helpless families, terrified by war, blinded their sons at birth in order to prevent them from becoming soldiers. Portugal's King John VI had died a few years earlier, leaving his wife, a brilliant and capable woman, to govern over inept courtiers. Their firstborn, groomed to take her place, had died in battle, and now the Queen Regent feared the day when another son, Dom Afonso, would claim the throne.

No attention had been paid to Dom Afonso, a sickly boy, who, at the age of six, had contracted a malignant fever, leaving him paralyzed on the right side and prone to fits of temper. Since he and his younger brother, Dom Pedro, were not intended to rule, they had received nothing in the way of education. Unable to read or write, the two brothers could barely sign their names.[1]

Dom Afonso spent his youth escaping from his tutor during the siesta, wandering the palace halls, peering out of windows, watching longingly as stall keepers' sons and local boys ran through the royal courtyard pelting stones at one another with little hand slings, damaging the palace shops along the way. Befriending the adolescents, Dom Afonso soon adopted their depraved ways, carousing through the streets of Lisbon at night, attacking innocent bystanders and indulging in illegal dogfights held by monks.

Desperate to break her son from these troublesome friendships, the queen moved Dom Afonso to another part of the palace and placed him under the constant care and watch of eighteen noblemen. One of them, Luis de Vasconcelos e Sousa, the count of Castelmelhor, not much older than Afonso, was recently returned from Italy, where he had been banished after accidentally killing a member of Dom Afonso's family. There, a fortune-teller had predicted that Castelmelhor would one day preside over Portugal. The count's unruly past, his natural good looks, and his congenial manner quickly won over the young monarch, and it was not long before Castelmelhor convinced Dom Afonso to divest the Queen Regent of her powers and relegate her to a convent. Having taken over, the nineteen-year-old King Dom Afonso VI named his new best friend clerk to the Crown, the highest position in the land after his own, and quickly returned to his debauched ways. Guided by the ambitious, inexperienced twenty-four-year-old Castelmelhor, Portugal faced almost certain ruin.

Before relinquishing her powers, the Queen Regent managed to broker two crucial alliances. She married off her only daughter to the king of England, Charles Stuart II. The dowry included two million pieces of gold, the city ports of Tangiers and Bombay (now Mumbai), as well as coffers of black tea that would become a staple of the English way of life. In exchange, she asked for ships and armies. Charles had little to send, but England's newly formed ties with the Portuguese would prove instrumental to Portugal's future.

The queen next turned to France, but the Treaty of the Pyrenees (1659)[2] forbade France from intervening in the Portuguese war, and France officially refused assistance. Henri de La Tour d'Auvergne, viscount of Turenne, minister of war, however, secretly agreed to help. Turenne, a Protestant and deeply religious man, felt Louis XIV had lost too much territory with the signing of the peace and disagreed with the treaty. The Portuguese war held the double advantage of keeping the Spanish busy and away from French borders, while France recovered from its losses, still providing an opportunity to train the next generation of French soldiers. Turenne believed that peace could only be maintained if France was in possession of the best and biggest army in the world, and that the best way to train his men was on foreign territory. Pressuring Louis XIV, Turenne secretly enlisted a friend and fellow Protestant, a German general Frederic Armand, Count of Schomberg, who had moved to France to serve under the recently anointed King Louis XIV.

Like Turenne, Schomberg was intensely religious and part of a growing number of military men who thought it important to treat their subordinates with respect and decency. He was known for being fair and generous; his loyalty was beyond doubt and his skills unsurpassed. Greatly respected, Schomberg's strength lay in his ability to lead small armies to victory. His skills were ideally suited to Portugal's needs and, added to this, Schomberg's German nationality would prevent Spain from accusing Louis XIV of breaking the terms of the treaty, leaving France free to secretly assist Portugal.

A man of few words, Schomberg was extremely civil, always obliging, and possessed an unwavering sense of integrity. He was of medium build, had good skin, and was said to be handsome. He was extremely particular about his grooming and was not adverse to flattery. A great believer in the virtues of military hierarchy, he excelled at strategy, and his assessments of men and situations were rarely wrong.[3]

He arrived in 1661 to find the Portuguese army in shambles. The Fidalgos saw no virtue in respecting authority. They considered themselves above the law and did not see why they should obey orders. Portuguese generals were paid according to merit. This encouraged endless deliberations, and the generals refused to commit to any decisive course of action for fear the wrong decision might lose them favor with the king. Decisions were taken based on superstitions and whims rather than on solid maxims of war. Portuguese troops were no better. With wages seldom paid, little if any loyalty existed among the men and battalions disbanded for no reason. Logistics were equally haphazard. Officers spent days bickering over who best deserved to camp near water wells, and by the time the army convened, the opportunity for battle had, more often than not, come and gone.

Over the course of the next three years, Schomberg taught the Portuguese soldiers how to march and camp in formation and how to conduct sieges, winning key battles along the way. The men remained difficult to handle and Schomberg requested help from Turenne. France sent troops composed mainly of ruffians who had been coerced into signing up over pints of beer and promises of riches. Disheartened by the lack of support, tired of the endless infighting, and doubtful that the inexperienced Castelmelhor knew what he was doing, Schomberg asked to return to France and Castelmelhor, jealous of Schomberg's successes, advised the king to let him go.

Schomberg was on the dock, his horses already on board the ship due to take him home to France, when a royal summons arrived asking him to stay.

Unbeknownst to Schomberg, a council of twenty-four artisans composed of the most upright men in the nation, whose purpose was to act in the best interest of the people of Portugal, had interceded on their behalf, urging the king to change his mind. Created by the ancient kings of Portugal in an effort to protect the morals of the population, the Council of Twenty-four knew that without Schomberg to guide the army, Spain would soon reclaim power over the Portuguese. Even the king needed to heed the advice of the council.

Schomberg agreed to stay under one condition. He wanted the best France had to offer. He needed experienced soldiers, gifted riders, and expert marksmen. An envoy was urgently dispatched. Under Turenne's direct orders, secret levies were raised in order to pay for the troops, and French commanders Maret and baron Henri Briquemault, Seigneur of Saint-Loup, were asked to enlist three hundred men each. Help was on its way.

HENRI BRIQUEMAULT, A FELLOW PROTESTANT AND FRIEND, SHARED Schomberg and Turenne's views on war. He made it his duty to know his men intimately, treated them with respect and chose every officer personally. He did not have to look far. The peace treaty had left a whole generation of young noblemen without employment. The army was not yet administered by the state. Noblemen owned their regiments and sold their services to the highest bidder. The Treaty of the Pyrenees, however, barred French regiments from fighting the Portuguese war and the companies were disbanded shortly after it was signed. Fiery young Frenchmen were forced to stay at home, while Irish, Italian, German, Swiss, and British regiments converged on Portugal.

Turenne's plan was illegal, but the officers did not care. The military was the only profession open to them. Laws designed to separate aristocracy from commoners forbade any employment other than war under penalty of losing their birthrights, including their exemption from paying taxes. These men needed to fight, if only to restore their sense of self-worth. They readily agreed to be stripped of their military ranks to become rogue agents. This subterfuge prevented Spain from claiming foul play. France would pay the officers generous wages in secret, and Louis XIV added promises of promotions once they returned.

Sometime in late December or early January 1664, a French ship set sail as the sun was rising over the icy French port of La Rochelle. Its official port of call was Ireland but, below deck, three hundred officers smuggled in during the previous night crowded the ship's hull supposedly filled with merchandise. Their true destination was Portugal. Most of the men knew each other as friends, relatives, or social acquaintances. All shared a passion for war. The keenest among them was a young nobleman by the name of Chamilly.

Noël Bouton, count of Saint-Léger and of Saint-Denis, marquis of Chamilly, was, according to his contemporaries, exceedingly handsome, loyal to a fault, unusually tall, and would have had to bend his head in order to avoid hitting the beams of the frigate. Henri Briquemault, Chamilly's commanding officer, lived some sixty miles from the Chamilly family homestead. Briquemault was friendly with Chamilly's father, and had witnessed Chamilly's strength of character and determination as a young man.

The Chamilly family belonged to the French province of Burgundy, governed by an extremely powerful prince. Louis II of Bourbon, prince of Condé, was known as the Great Condé. Chamilly's father, Nicolas, and his older brother, Herard, had spent their lives at the service of the Great Condé. Herard had acted as the Great Condé's page since the age of nine and was now a rising star in Condé's army. Chamilly was expected to follow in his brother's footsteps but circumstances led Chamilly in a different direction.

France was still an amalgamation of different dukedoms and the Great Condé aspired to owning more than Burgundy. Derisive, insolent, unyielding, vindictive, proud, miserly, and a bad husband, the Great Condé was also known as the greatest general of France. He never bathed and a cloud of flies constantly swirled around him. Spurred on by his elder sister, Anne Geneviève de Bourbon Condé, and encouraged by his younger brother, Armand Bourbon, prince of Conti, the Great Condé decided to carve a piece of France for himself.

Anne Geneviève, the eldest of the three, was said to be the most beautiful woman in France. Trapped in a loveless marriage to Henri II de Orléans, duke of Longueville, she led a tumultuous life, collecting lovers along the way. Together with her present lover, François, duke of La Rochefoucauld, she was greatly responsible for convincing the rest of the French aristocracy to defy the Crown. Chamilly's father being under the patronage of the Great Condé, the Chamilly family suddenly found itself an enemy of France.[4]

Chamilly was fourteen years old when Anne Geneviève and other aristocrats fleeing from an angry king arrived in Stenay, a Condé stronghold governed by Chamilly's father. Anne Geneviève took an instant dislike to the elder Chamilly and set about to destroy him. She may well have succeeded were it not for the intervention of Turenne, who, secretly in love with the stunning and charismatic Anne Geneviève, had followed her into exile. Turenne was unlike the Great Condé in every way. He was universally loved and respected. Genuinely kind, he took care of his men and treated them fairly. Turenne's presence in Stenay was short-lived. Realizing his mistake, Turenne had left the aristocratic uprising, known as the Fronde, to rejoin France in its efforts to unite, but the few months Turenne had spent living in the Condé stronghold had been enough to make a deep and lasting impression on the young Chamilly. Turenne's actions had taught Chamilly that respect carried a man further than disdain and that soldiers make their best efforts when treated as human beings. These lessons would remain with Chamilly for the rest of his life and on the day of his eighteenth birthday, leaving his beloved family behind, Chamilly had enlisted under Turenne in Louis XIV's army to fight against the Great Condé. Chamilly now faced his brother and father on opposite sides of the political divide.

The aristocrats eventually relented and being the astute politician that he was, Louis XIV saw the virtues of making friends with the princes of France and offered the Great Condé and his followers complete amnesty. Chamilly's father returned to France and to the family domain a poor and broken man. Sensing their father was not long for this world, Herard, the eldest son, decided to settle down and find a wife.[5] Chamilly, deeply relieved to see his family reunited, willingly handed what little assets and titles he owned over to Herard in order to help him secure a good match. Chamilly kept only two crumbling castles that provided no income. Like all the other young aristocrats in his position, peace had left Chamilly without a job. Profoundly uninterested in administrative tasks, Chamilly longed to return to the battlefield.

Chamilly personified all the virtues extolled by Briquemault, Schomberg, and Turenne. He lived to serve his king, he favored the greater good over personal gain, he was honorable and courageous. An unquenchable passion for war propelled the young Chamilly forward and echoes of Schomberg's glorious Portuguese battles were more than enough to compel him to join Briquemault's covert mission. Chamilly readily agreed to leave the lofty hills of Burgundy for the incandescent plains of an unknown Portugal.

Briquemault's secret invitation created a golden opportunity for the young soldier. Peace had caught Chamilly too early in his career. The Portuguese war would be Chamilly's chance to prove his worth. Briquemault's offer provided him with a long awaited sense of purpose, the chance to win a regiment, and with any amount of luck, help get him back afloat financially. Portugal's illustrious past only added to the thrill of wanting to defend it.

When Chamilly handed over the papers forgoing his rank in the French army on a blustery January morning, the quiet irreverence of his gaze must have hinted at the brilliant and difficult future that awaited him. During his lifetime, Chamilly would become the most famous man of France. However, for now, his presence on the clandestine ship was, like that of every young man around him, crucial to his financial survival and fueled by romantic notions of brilliance and glory.

Violent winds sent waves crashing over the bow and seasick officers must have struggled to sustain images of future greatness. A few weeks into their voyage, somewhere off the coast of Cork, Portuguese buccaneers attacked the little

French frigate. The pirates were, in fact, Portuguese sailors under the employ of King Dom Afonso, posing as mercenaries in order to fool the Spanish, with orders to smuggle the French soldiers into Lisbon. The officers boarded the Portuguese galleon the *San Luis* in the dead of the night. Contrary winds delayed the ship by several weeks, but the vessel finally dropped anchor in the port of Lisbon sometime at the beginning of 1664.[6]

Fireworks greeted the French officers. Carnival was at its height. The startling whiteness of Lisbon's houses pierced the grayness of a new year's light. Lively banners hung from windows. The smell of exotic spices permeated the air. Bull runs took place through city streets, and brightly colored ribbons graced church altars while nuns offered pastries as gifts. The romantic, melancholic lament of the fado, Portugal's soulful music, echoed through Lisbon's streets, mixing African and Arab rhythms. Masked revelers, attired in beautifully unfamiliar costumes, greeted the strangers. Lent was around the corner, and the Portuguese would make merry until Ash Wednesday.

Here in Portugal, Fidalgos treated servants as equals, traded slaves, slept with whores, spent their time in prayer or died of love. For these young French noblemen used to the rigid hierarchy of France, the Portuguese's passion, their disrespect for rules, and their lust for pleasure must have struck odd chords of fancy and confusion. After weeks spent cramped in the hulls of a frigate, how strange it must have felt to enter a world where the king lived depraved, where life was exalted, and where love reigned paramount. It may have also been strangely beguiling.

CHAMILLY'S MILITARY TITLE WAS IMMEDIATELY REINSTATED AND HE was provided with a horse to travel to the small town of Aldeia Galega to be outfitted with harnesses and muskets. The horses had been difficult to come by, and the French diplomat, Jean Jacob Frémont d'Ablancourt, Schomberg's representative at court (as well as friend, trusted adviser, and right-hand man), had haggled to get them. Mules transported the artillery, ammunition, and the food to the general headquarters in Estremoz. Built entirely of white marble, Estremoz was ideally located to pursue missions north of the border.

The remainder of the French officers arrived, as did an English regiment known for its ferociousness.[7] The French and the English combined (three hundred French officers and one hundred and fifty British) would oversee the fifteen thousand Portuguese soldiers. Under Castelmelhor's insistence, the Fidalgos chose a Portuguese general to command over Schomberg. Pressured by France, Schomberg reluctantly agreed to Castelmelhor's terms.

Two months after his arrival, Chamilly was appointed captain[8] of one of Briquemault's regiments. The commis-

sion was drawn up on April 30, 1664, at the general head-
quarters in Estremoz, and was dictated by Schomberg him-
self. The document reads: "Taking into account the valor,
experience, and capabilities of Monsieur the Count of
Chamilly-Saint-Léger, proof of which he gave during the
French wars, he is hereby appointed captain of cavalry in
Colonel Briquemault's regiment." At the same time, in
France, a similar document was being secretly ratified.
Chamilly had turned twenty-eight years old a few days
earlier.

Much marching and countermarching took place during Chamilly's first campaign. Due to the inhospitable climate, campaigns were short and occurred only twice a
year, once in the springtime and then again in the autumn.
The Portuguese, whose bread was paid for by the king,
complained they were not given enough. Schomberg advanced money from his personal funds in order to keep
the Portuguese soldiers willing to fight.

The newly reconfigured Portuguese army went mostly un-
defeated until the very end when Chamilly's garrison town,
Cabeça de Vide, came under Spanish attack. The slaughter
took place at night while the men slept. Crammed next to
each other, sleeping on the ground without mattresses or
bedding, the men never woke up as the finely crafted Spanish rapiers silently pierced through their bodies.

Two hundred prisoners were taken; the rest were killed
or dispersed. That night, only twenty-six men managed

to escape, Chamilly among them. Corraling the horses, Chamilly fled a city in flames, taking with him two Portuguese flags. The number of flags helped determine the winner at the end of a battle or war. They were a small compensation. Countless men and horses were lost. Chamilly's first campaign had lasted only a short six or seven weeks.

Summer, with its sweltering heat, came and went. The autumn campaign was spent fortifying a border town taken from the Spanish. Briquemault's men worked the better part of September erecting wooden barricades and securing strategic positions, and unless Frémont d'Ablancourt could find something else for his special forces to do, he looked at paying the French officers a year's salary for two months worth of work.

D'Ablancourt also needed to find a way to lift Schomberg's spirits. Castelmelhor's aversion to decision making and the constant insubordination coming from the Portuguese commanders left Schomberg teetering on the verge of depression. The French diplomat suggested that Schomberg attack a small coastal town on the Gulf of Cadiz that faced Tangiers. Protected by forty Spanish soldiers housed in a crumbling castle, the quaint fishing town of Ayamonte provided access to the Atlantic and would create an invaluable port of call for Portuguese ships looking to drop anchor before the last stretch to Lisbon. It would also address the pressing issue of housing unwelcome foreign troops.

The general population was responsible for supplying

foreign troops with lodgings, food, and tending to the soldiers when wounded. The soldiers were largely ungrateful
and unruly, and the Portuguese were starting to refuse to
take them in. Capturing Ayamonte would alleviate pres-
sures on the population and create a Portuguese stronghold
within Spanish territory. Excited, Schomberg propelled his
men into action at the beginning of 1665. Small formations
traveled to various rendezvous points, from which they were
handed secret instructions to convene in Beja, Mariana's
home town.

Chamilly must have welcomed the distraction. His
youngest brother had passed away a few months earlier,
killed at sea by a cannon ball while onboard a ship in
pursuit of pirates. With grief close at hand, Chamilly cantered through the white pallor of the vacant Portuguese
landscape on a land so flat, the horizon appeared to bend
and break where the sky met the earth. Nothing here
evoked Chamilly's beloved Burgundy, strewn with beautiful castles built on mountainsides overrun by luscious
vines laden with grapes. Protected by large felt hats,
draped in long black capes covering parts of their
mounts, the men passed through endless harvested fields
of wheat in a continuum of rain interspersed with flurries
of snow.

Beja's marble tower rose above the plains, cutting a decisive figure against the fading sky. It was not long before
rows of tents appeared at the outskirts of town. The men

settled in for what they expected would be a stay of several weeks while their superiors planned and plotted the attack.

Among those present to meet the soldiers was the nobleman Rui de Melo, who belonged to one of Beja's most prestigious families. Francisco, Mariana's father, had selected Rui de Melo as his son-in-law, but Melo had proven a disappointment to Francisco. Chosen for his connections, the rough and uncultured Melo had fallen ill at the start of the marriage, convalescing at the Alcoforado estate for close to five years while refusing to do any work. He had finally left, after borrowing money from Mariana's father, to set himself up raising livestock. The debt remained unpaid. The pig farmer spent most of his time at war away from Ana, and he, like many others, preferred frequenting convent gates to spending time with his wife.

Mariana was about to turn twenty-five. The previous year had been filled with sorrow. The wonderfully wise abbess, Madre Maria de Mendonca, Mariana's tutor, who loved Mariana as a daughter and had helped her navigate the complexities of convent life, passed away. Mariana's mother followed a few months later, leaving behind a little girl of three. The rift between Francisco and Ana's husband must have been significant because Francisco put the child in Mariana's care, an unusual choice given that Ana already had four children and was capable of providing the child with a home. Bending the rules as only he could, Francisco entrusted the little Maria to his favorite daughter. Unlike

Mariana, who had kept her name, Maria underwent the customary religious renaming and took on the name of Perigrina. Mariana would act as mother and tutor to Perigrina until she was twelve and old enough to enter the novitiate.

Over the years, Mariana had come to occupy a central position as scribe for the convent's administrative affairs. Her responsibilities included ordering goods like soap or salt, necessary for the upkeep of the convent and the welfare of the nuns, as well as overseeing real estate transactions. The few examples of her writing that survive show a hand that exudes strength and simplicity. The ink flows evenly; seldom is a correction made or a word blotted. She signs her name in full, Mariana Alcoforado, disregarding the common appellation of Madre. Most probably, Mariana was being groomed to become abbess, and though this was never to be, she, in turn, prepared Perigrina, who eventually did take on the position.

A large opening called the window of Mertola carved directly into the stone of the convent's wall led to a terrace from which the nuns viewed the southern plains.[9] The window opened onto a large unencumbered horizon similar to that of Mariana's childhood and in the early days of February 1665, Mariana and her companions would have noticed large billows of smoke hovering over the plains. Lit in the early morning, the fires signaled the presence of soldiers standing near bushels of arms trying to shield themselves from the cold. Privy to political secrets because of her connections, Mariana knew that the commanding officers were French noblemen come to help win the war. The young nun and the officer stood only a few miles apart, both unaware that their paths were about to cross.

The men had been gathered only a few days when d'Ablancourt cancelled the operation. Castelmelhor, secretly engaged in peace talks with Spain, had forced him to countermand Schomberg's plans. Disgruntled, the men were ordered back to headquarters.

INCENSED BY THE COUNTERORDER, SCHOMBERG ASKED TO LEAVE. The Council of Twenty-four intervened once more. An emotionally drained Schomberg begrudgingly agreed to stay. The animosity between the general and the king's clerk reached new heights. Schomberg fell ill. Castelmelhor was beginning to question the value of the French altogether when a troubling turn of events forced him to reconsider; a rumor suggesting King Dom Afonso was impotent had begun circulating.

The young king, busy partaking in various acts of debauchery, spent nights in the company of whores. Bored with a twelve-year-old girl he had sequestered and christened the infanta, he entered into a relationship with a Dominican nun. His extravagances[10] grew in parallel with the rumor of his impotence. Castelmelhor decided that the time had come to marry him off. Necessity overriding pride, he made his way to Schomberg's lodgings after supper one night to enlist Schomberg's help. Three hours later, he had what he wanted.

Portuguese diplomats were dispatched to broker the king's wedding. A bidding took place between France and England. After much deliberation and many failed attempts, Castelmelhor chose the French princess Marie-Françoise, Isabelle de Savoie, duchess of Aumale, princess of Nemours. An arresting nineteen-year-old blonde, Marie-Françoise's incandescent beauty masked a fierce ambition. Her will to overcome Dom Afonso's shortcomings in favor of the Portuguese Crown should have served as a warning to Castelmelhor. But the porcelain medallion and the painted portraits sent to help was Dom Afonso spoke of innocence and youth and Castelmelhor believed he would rule over her as he did his king.

Directing his energies toward marrying off the king, burried under yards of fabric in anticipation of the momentous event, Castelmelhor did not notice that Spain prepared for war. Warned by Schomberg that the Spanish had hired experienced Swiss and German regiments with the intention of attacking Portugal, Castelmelhor, convinced his peace negotiations were succeeding, ignored him. The May campaign of 1665 was barely underway when Spain undertook its most daring move yet.

FIFTEEN THOUSAND SPANISH SOLDIERS INVADED THE ALENTEJO ON June 10, 1665, attacking the beloved homestead of Dom Afonso's father. Considered the jewel of Portugal, it was believed that if Villa Viçosa fell, so would the rest of Portugal. A tiny infantry, trapped in the city's castle, valiantly held up for six days before falling on June 16, providing barely enough time for the Portuguese army to assemble. Converging from every part of the country, the provinces finally banded together. The battle of Monte Claros, as it would eventually be called, was ferocious and decisive.

Schomberg led a band of mismatched men, some dressed in formal attire as if going to a ball, wearing silk stockings and garters, while others walked barefoot with threadbare jackets thrown over their shoulders taken from dead or dying soldiers.[11] The men carried antiquated arms that barely held a charge and few knew what they were doing. They faced twenty-two Spanish squadrons clad in black helmets, sporting shiny breastplates, and armed with the most modern weaponry available.

Filled with confusion, craftsmanship, and ingenuity, the battle lasted eight hours. Swords were quickly abandoned as the soldiers collected stones from crumbling walls to bludgeon each other to death. At one point, Schomberg himself dismounted, grabbed a pike, and started plunging the blade between the legs of the enemy horses, teaching the Portuguese how to irritate the horses' hooves, forcing the horses into fits that threw the riders to the ground. Soon a thousand riderless horses cantered toward Estremoz, and misguided Portuguese soldiers fled, sending dispatches to Lisbon announcing the Portuguese had lost. They were greatly mistaken.

Schomberg spent the next hours systematically attacking the Spanish, squadron by squadron. Chamilly and the six hundred Frenchmen pushed the enemy into a valley that followed the edge of an olive grove. Forced in amongst the trees, the Spanish cavalry scattered. Their commander was shot down. Fifteen hundred Spaniards fled across the border. The Portuguese tried to pursue them, but the horses refused to go any further. The battle was over. The Portuguese had won against extraordinary odds.

When day broke on the morning following the battle, Chamilly was among the thousands who greeted Schomberg to the sound of drums, trumpets, and lengthy clamors of admiration. Eighty-six Spanish flags and eighteen standards firmly planted on the ground surrounded Schomberg's tent. A sea of Spanish helmets dangled at the ends of pikes. The entire army fell silent as the flap of Schomberg's tent was lifted and the general stepped forward. One after another, Chamilly and his fellow officers offered congratulations. Never had there been such a glorious and short campaign: twenty-four hours, in which the Portuguese had fought, won, and come home to sleep. Four thousand Spaniards were killed and wounded. The German squadrons, who had been hired by the Spanish to finish off the Portuguese army, enlisted under Schomberg's command that same day.[12]

THE POPULATION OF LISBON WENT MAD WITH JOY. FOR THE FIRST time in over twenty years, victory suddenly seemed within Portugal's grasp. Schomberg was appointed governor general of the province of Alentejo in honor of the battle. His first task was to promote his men. Chamilly was named field master and captain of the first company of a cavalry regiment on December 7, 1665. Henceforth, eighty cavalrymen would fight under his command, and he would answer directly to Briquemault.

Schomberg's next consideration was his soldiers' precarious living conditions. Soldiers slept on floors. Sanitary conditions were foul. The men froze in winter and suffered through unbearable summers. Used shoes were not replaced. The Crown supplied the men with bread and barley only. Betting was insidious. Money came sporadically, and salaries were rarely paid on time, if at all, and the unruliness of the troops further alienated the Portuguese populations. Without improvements, Schomberg faced possible defections and irreparable damage to local relations.

Having fought mostly north of the border, Schomberg decided to move his men south, towards the heart and soul of Spain, near the undulating hills of Andalusia. Chamilly received orders that, starting in March, he would be garrisoned in Beja.

3

LOVE, A MATTER
OF HAPPENSTANCE

"In love what is the greatest crime, to be refused or not have dared to ask?"

MARQUIS DE SOURDIS, *THIRTY-TWO QUESTIONS ON LOVE*,
CIRCA 1664 FOR THE SALON OF THE MARQUISE DE SABLÉ

"I had never known incessant praises before yours . . . everyone spoke in your favor."

MARIANA ALCOFORADO, Letter 5

Y NOW, CHAMILLY AND HIS COMPANIONS WERE FA-
mous. Noirmontier, Balandry, Chevri, Chauvet,
Chamilly—the mere mention of these names
suggested an aura of invincibility. As the officers prepared to move to Beja, French vessels arrived in the
port of Lisbon confirming King Dom Afonso's upcoming
marriage with the princess of Nemours.[1] Carnival was under way, and the nuns looked forward to welcoming the
officers.

Preparations had barely begun when unexpected news
arrived, informing the convent that the Queen Regent was
dying. Decorations were set aside. All thoughts turned
toward the extraordinary woman who had guided Portugal

in its darkest hour. Portugal owed the queen its most inspired undertakings. She had convinced her husband to take the Crown and had brought the French to Portuguese shores. Now, removed from power, abandoned by her son, she lay in a convent that was more of a prison than a refuge.

Dom Afonso was in Salvaterra, a small town north of Lisbon where the court spent Carnival. Called to his mother's bedside, he delayed his departure, stopping for entertainment on the way. He reached Lisbon on February 27, only to find his mother no longer able to speak.

Bending forward, Dom Afonso kissed his mother's hand, asking for her blessing, while his younger brother, Dom Pedro, broke down in tears. Castelmelhor whispered something in Dom Afonso's ear, causing the king to rise and bid his mother adieu. Inconsolable, Dom Pedro was dragged away. An hour later she was dead.

A few days earlier, Marie-Françoise, the princess of Nemours, had contracted to marry Dom Afonso. The passing of one queen heralded the arrival of another.

News of the Queen Regent's death spread across the country within hours. Bells tolled night and day. Carnival garlands were replaced with heavy drapes of purple. Prayers rose from every altar, and Mariana's father and brothers departed for Lisbon to be present at the funeral. The convent parlors stopped receiving visitors.

The lead coffin lined with white silk, black velvet, and golden threads was carefully placed in a big chestnut box on a simple carriage pulled by mules whose heads were covered in black. A single white flag bearing the queen's coat of arms led the procession toward the fields of Santa Clara, where she would be buried next to the Carmelite church. Night fell, and lanterns were lit for the thousands who mourned her.

Profoundly affected by the loss of his only true ally, Schomberg fell ill. Proclamations were read in every municipality instructing the population on the bereavement procedure. Nine days of heavy mourning followed by six months of lighter grieving.

It was March 1666. Circumstances were about to bring the officer and the nun together for the first time. Scholars claim Mariana's description of her first encounter with Chamilly is borrowed from an ancient Latin poem called *Héroïdes.*[2] History provides a simpler explanation.

Barred from visiting the convents until further notice, Chamilly and the other officers took to exercising their horses in the southern fields of Beja, overlooked by the window of Mertola. Which nun or servant girl first noticed the cavalcades of the officers is today unknown, but according to Marianna's letters, the training became a daily attraction.

The soldiers wore colorful, varied, and shining clothing, some dressed in red, some in green, and some covered with multi-colored braiding. Uniforms did not yet exist, and the men spent as much if not more time deciding what to wear than women. Vests covered long flowing calico shirts. The men drew their hair back into ponytails and wore swash-buckler hats made of black felt, with large floppy rims decorated by long feathers, invented by the Portuguese to protect themselves from the sun.³ The Fidalgos wore long beards and little fashionable glasses that served no purpose other than to lend them, they believed, an intellectual air. The Frenchmen kept their faces clean-shaven.

In the weeks preceding Chamilly's official entrance into Mariana's life, an intricate dance between two strangers began. Chamilly was easily recognizable because of his height, and in her letters Mariana describes how she watched breathlessly as he cavorted with his companions, calling attention to his capers. By the time the appropriate period of mourning was over and the soldiers were invited to visit the parlors, the soon to turn twenty-six-year-old Mariana Alcoforado had fallen in love.

BALTHAZAR, MARIANA'S YOUNGER BROTHER AND LEGAL HEIR TO THE Alcoforado fortune, is believed to be the one responsible for Chamilly and Mariana meeting.⁴ Funny, impulsive, and brilliant, Balthazar grew up admiring his father and seeking to emulate him. Balthazar's exuberance was difficult to contain, and Francisco preferred his second son, Miguel, whose conservative and stern nature was closer to his own.

Miguel was less of a rebel rouser than Balthazar and Francisco, hoping to steer Balthazar toward religion, had placed his eldest son in a nearby monastery to study. According to his own stipulations, if Balthazar became a priest Francisco could legally hand over the estate to the younger Miguel. Rejecting his father's plan, Balthazar left the priory to enlist in the neighboring county of Niebla, and the twenty-one-year-old first met Chamilly on the second of January 1666, in the midst of battle at the edge of the small market town of Alguerie de la Puebla, a few miles into Andalusia.

Fires, lit along the town walls to deter the Portuguese from attacking, forced Chamilly and his men to smother the flames using their capes, creating a passage for the infantry. The Spanish, retreating to a fort that protected the main church, deluged the Portuguese infantry with bullets.

Balthazar, pushing to the front, exalted the infantry to protect the forty cavalrymen about to storm the fort. Backed up into the church itself, the Spanish soldiers surrendered. Ravenous pillaging ensued. Schomberg barred the churches from being plundered, ordering Chamilly, Balthazar, and others to protect them. The governor of Beja, Diogo Gomes de Figueiredo, impressed by Balthazar's bravery and skill, recounted the young man's exploits in a letter addressed to the king.

Word of the Portuguese victory spread. A governor surrendered his fortress within three hours of the battle taking place. He included his cavalry, provided he was spared. The horses were distributed among the officers of the troops. The young Alcoforado had made his mark. Chamilly's nascent friendship with Balthazar was about to lead him to Mariana.

THE RED HEELS OF THE FRENCH OFFICERS' DRESS SHOES CLICKED along the stone floors announcing their arrival. The clean-shaven officers wore powdered wigs and colored ribbons, French waistcoats with shiny buttons. Their bearded counterparts wore leather studded boots, clanging swords, and dark clothing.

The nuns invited the French officers to sit on long benches abutting the parlor walls. They offered the soldiers beautiful detailed paper cutouts featuring exotic birds from all over the world from peacocks to blue jays. Three dimensional paper flowers decorated pastries wrapped in fine tissue paper of pale blue and pink. These in turn were expertly shaped into different patterns, and presented on silver and iron trays. The French, famous for their interest in culinary matters even then, must have expressed genuine admiration and interest in knowing how much sugar, chocolate, sugar-coated almonds, eggs, and jam were used to create the candy boxes they were given to take home.[5]

The nuns made cases upon cases of marmalade, wonderful breads, and the boxes of candies were made dozens at a time.

The pastries served as emissaries, preparing the ground for delicate questions of money, favors to ask, and indulgences to seek. A certain trepidation must have accompanied the offer of the *trouxa de ovos* (egg fool) crowned by a delicate paper rose and considered the best in the country, and the Portuguese soldiers may well have laughed at the Frenchmen unaccustomed to eating such delicacies. One special cake was not served that day. Usually reserved for newlyweds, the nuns sometimes served it with something else in mind, for it was called the *cake of love*.

The rigor of the Franciscan habit with its regular black damask was, at Concieção, replaced with silks that came from Europe or India, the roughness transformed into a sensuous flutter. The hems of the nuns' skirts were slightly raised. Few finished goods were manufactured in Portugal, and the delicate shoes observed under the nuns' habits came from abroad. Intricately laced underwear layered the inner folds of the nuns' habits, making the fabric flow. The nuns had inherited the Muslim practice of wearing luxurious dresses covered in ribbons and jewelry under their religious attire, hiding a world inside a world.

The rough piece of rope meant to wrap around the nuns' waists was replaced with silk ribbons that came from Italy. The use of ribbons was so extravagant that a law was passed in 1668 to restrict men and women to fifty-five meters of ribbons each, per garment. Amidst this quiver of cloth, the nuns secretly vied for potential patrons.

How tempting to imagine Mariana and Chamilly's first meeting. Her letters let us guess at a woman unaware of her beauty. Her station in life would have left her less interested in material goods. Her religious habit might have been less encumbered, her gait more equal and modest, the simplicity of her manner more affecting for Chamilly than all the fineries that came before her.

Portuguese scholars have speculated that it is possible Balthazar wanted to use his sister's French skills to be able to converse at greater lengths with Chamilly. We know for certain that the dashing young captain was introduced as the Count of Saint-Léger, the name he chose to use during his stay in Portugal.

We can only anticipate the imperceptible start. The mundaneness of the conversation as pulses raced a little faster, officer and nun surprised at how easily circumstances brought them together. Safe in their designated role as hostess and guest, surrounded by a multitude of people, their meeting was sanctioned by society. Chamilly was at the height of his fame, hailed by Mariana's friends and family as a savior of her country. She was the daughter of one of the most respected men of Portugal.

Not much was needed for Chamilly and Mariana to discover they shared birthdays in April, or that his sisters were also nuns, that he had recently lost a brother, and she, her mother. Threads of recognition, often the catalyst to love, may well have been woven over tea and Portuguese pastries.

Chamilly was immersed in a culture that bore very little resemblance to his own. He lived far from anyone who knew him, in a world where love, courtship, and wooing operated under completely different rules.

A MONTH AFTER MARIANA AND CHAMILLY HAD OFFICIALLY MET, Schomberg called on his cavalry and four thousand foot soldiers to attack one of the richest municipalities of Andalusia, the town of Saint-Lucar situated below Mertola on the Guadiana River. Chamilly and Balthazar departed on May 29, 1666. The town resisted three days before surrendering. Portuguese troops had never been seen in this area. Another village was ransacked and burned. The short expeditions instilled such fear in the people that unfortified villages and castles bought their way out of pillaging. These "contributions" were divided between the officers and the cavalrymen. News of Schomberg's victories arrived in Lisbon before Castelmelhor even knew he had gone. Far from being grateful, Castelmelhor declared it was not in Portugal's interest to conduct the war in Andalusia. Lack of bread sent the soldiers back to their quarters. Chamilly spent the stifling summer months in Beja dividing his days between hunts, games, exercising the horses, and spending his afternoons in the company of Mariana.

WHILE CHAMILLY CLIMBED THE BARRICADES OF SAINT-LUCAR, THE young Marie-Françoise, future queen of Portugal, was busy taking her leave from the court of France. She and Mariana would never meet, yet Marie-Françoise's future love would preside over Mariana's fate.

The marriage contract between Dom Afonso and Marie-Françoise stipulated that the wedding occur in London, but the plague was raging through the English capital, and instead, the nuptials took place by proxy on Sunday morning, June 27, 1666, in the small port town of La Rochelle, France. While the bride waited in the room next door, two old men representing Marie-Françoise and Dom Afonso knelt down to be blessed in a tiny white chapel and were wed.

Raised in a convent after her father was killed in a duel by her uncle, reared to dance and converse brilliantly, Marie-Françoise's education was geared toward the ornamental rather than the practical. She had a good knowledge of history and letters and though she had initially welcomed the match, in the months preceding the betrothal, doubts had taken hold of her. Rumors of Dom Afonso's impotence had reached her, which added to tales of his perverseness. Portuguese manners and ways were constantly being described in unflattering terms and now, as if to confirm her worst fears, there she stood, on the eve of her departure, clothed in her finest apparel, forbidden from witnessing her own wedding.

At the end of the ceremony, the elderly Portuguese states-man saluted a recalcitrant twenty-year-old Queen. Marie-Françoise's official mission was to bring the two countries closer together; her secret instructions were to keep the war effort alive. Her sense of dread was overwhelming.

A heavy fog detained the convoy longer than antici-pated.[6] Marie-Françoise was sick before they had even left the harbor. She desperately pleaded with the captain to leave her on an island or take her back to La Rochelle, but the winds turned and the ship set sail on the fourth of July, a week after she had wed. Heavy fog settled in and the voy-age took thirty-two days. Marie-Françoise would never see French shores again.

The convent of Concieção devoted June and July of 1666 to the future queen's arrival. Extra flour was ordered. Con-cieção was famous for its large pastries weighing up to thirty-five pounds. Orders for the desserts had already come from the capital in anticipation of the royal nuptials. Secu-rity was organized to protect the pastries from being stolen en route to Lisbon. Inadvertently, the wedding preparations must have spurred unintended dialogue. The excitement surrounding the event facilitated Mariana and Chamilly's courtship. The marriage festivities themselves would play an important part in bringing the officer and the nun closer together.

The arrival of Marie-Françoise in the port of Lisbon cap-tured the imagination of every woman in the country be she young or old, celibate or married. Crowds gathered early in the morning to welcome their new queen. Dom Afonso, however, set off late in the afternoon, begrudgingly accompanied by his brother, Dom Pedro. The two men were at odds with each other since the death of their mother, and Dom Pedro had reluctantly agreed to come.

A small sculpted boat, pulled by fifteen men dressed in liveries of red and gold, carried the brothers. They sat on crimson cushions lined with golden fringes underneath a velvet awning surrounded by richly woven drapes. Etiquette required that Marie-Françoise wait below deck in her chamber. The queen, upon seeing the king, sank to her knees. It is unclear whether Marie-Françoise knelt out of shock or deference.[7] Dom Afonso's last two years of absolute depravity, encouraged by Castelmelhor, had turned him into a short stout man of twenty-three, whose bulk was increased by his wearing six or seven layers of coats and waistcoats atop a thick metal vest. His fear of colds meant he always wore three or four caps and hats, one on top of the other. His hair and tone were fair, and he might have been handsome had he not suffered from a bad skin condition that forced him to bathe twice a day. The young king, covered in blemishes, barely able to move in his clothing, also endeavored to kneel, but he stumbled instead and was caught by his gentlemen-in-waiting. Had he succeeded, historians surmise he would not have been able to stand again.

Marie-Françoise was a sophisticated twenty-year-old who had spent much time exposed to all kinds of depravity at

Louis XIV's court. She had witnessed aristocrats spitting on parquet floors and was used to the smells of nobles and servants defecating in hallways and stairwells.[8] Nothing, however, had prepared her for the little fat man with a charge of snuff up his nose who took her by the hand. Behind him stood his brother, Dom Pedro. Tall and handsome, he bore no deformity, was extremely well-spoken, and possessed a modest air that was unusual in people of his rank. While the king gingerly led his bride toward the barge, onlookers say that more than once, Marie-Françoise cast a furtive glance in Dom Pedro's direction.[9]

Marie-Françoise must have sensed the tension between Dom Afonso and his nineteen-year-old brother. No sooner had they touched ground than Dom Pedro made excuses and retired to a friend's house. Dom Afonso and his new wife proceeded to Alcantara, the king's vacation home, a short distance outside Lisbon. There, Dom Afonso and Marie-Françoise spent a few hours by themselves. She contracted a headache shortly thereafter, and Dom Afonso would wait three days before re-entering her bedchamber. Their married life was off to an inauspicious start.

MARIANA'S FATHER WAS INVITED TO TAKE PART IN THE PROCESSION marking the queen's official entry in Lisbon. He brought his sons, including Miguel, who was friendly with Dom

Pedro. The French commander Maret, whose men were also stationed in Beja, was incensed to discover that the queen had no royal guard and volunteered his men for the task. He went so far as to pay for the officers' liveries, so they could serve as Marie-Françoise's escort. Brique-mault, Chamilly's commander, also attended the festivities with some of his men, leaving Chamilly in charge and alone in Beja.

The sun shone bright when at midday, on August 25, 1666, the new queen took her place in the royal carriage to the left of Dom Afonso. She faced Dom Pedro and the principal lady-in-waiting, the mother of Castelmelhor. Crowds looked on as the members and officers of the national assembly headed the procession to the sounds of trumpets. Men rode opulently attired horses. Royal staff bearers, heralds, and judges, dressed in their robes of office, Mariana's father among them, followed. Coaches filled with nobility seated in order of rank came before the magnificent royal carriage. Maret's guard brought up the rear.

Historians recount that the young queen kept staring at Dom Pedro. Cloaked in black as the custom demanded, the prince wore a long black peruke and a long lace band. Shy in crowds, Dom Pedro spoke very little and appeared generally uneasy as the procession traveled under beautiful arches erected by different foreign nations.

The people cheered at the roar of artillery and cried for joy as the new queen and Dom Afonso, helped by a myriad of servants, knelt in the cathedral, listening religiously to the *Te Deum* sung in their honor. As bells chimed from every corner of the country, the good people of Portugal did not realize that the inklings of love forming in the queen's heart were not for the king, her husband, but for the prince, her brother-in-law.

BELLS TOLLED IN BEJA CALLING THE MEN TO ARMS. WHILE FRANcisco Alcoforado prepared to don his judicial robes, the Spanish were quietly moving their troops into Portuguese territory. Beja was about to be attacked.

Chamilly, left to guard the city while Briquemault was away, ordered the convents secured. Nuns feared rape more than pillaging, and the convents must have welcomed the protection offered by Chamilly and his men. The window of Mertola faced south toward Spain, and offered a strategic advantage. Chamilly could only get to the window from the inside.

It is impossible to tell what Chamilly felt as he left the panicked tumult of the streets to enter the hushed tones of the convent of Conci, Crossing the threshold of Mariana's private world, the unexpected greeted him. Hers was a universe entirely of women, rounded and opulent, more pagan than saint, filled with mystery and elegance. A singular silence permeated the walls. Probably guided by the abbess, the men made their way through the convent's main quadrant, walking over tiled stones under which deceased nuns lay buried. They passed through richly decorated chapels where peach-colored sculptures of half-naked women stared down at the men, their arms raised above their heads displaying lavish breasts with nipples the color of fresh-picked apples. More figures of naked women adorned the columns like prows on ships. A virgin breastfed baby Jesus. Flickering candlelight called the figures to life. An overwhelming sensuality seeped from curved arches, flowing in and out of one another. Fresh smells of gold dust mixed in with paint and soiled rags left behind on empty scaffolds conveyed the haste of fleeing workers.

The rustle of cloth and the hurried footsteps of nuns scattering before the men must have added to the overwhelming impression of an untold presence. Careful female eyes watched from shadowy recesses as the soldiers passed through narrow hallways and climbed the darkened staircases to the outer walls. Men stayed at the window readying their muskets.

The convent hid sumptuous gardens filled with trees and flowering shrubs. Carefully nestled among the greenery stood the nuns' houses built independently from the dormitories and adorned with ornate wooden doors and windows, little paths led to them, and somewhere in one of these houses lived Mariana.

The convent door closed behind Chamilly, delivering

him to the sun's harsh light. Squinting, the officer must have looked upward toward his men posted on the terraces, perhaps taking in for the first time the convent gargoyles, still visible today. They depict nuns crouching, their habits gathered around their calves as if giving birth, silently screaming.[10]

Scholars trying to dispel the possibility of the affair have maintained that a man of Chamilly's probity would never have stepped beyond the parlor walls. Symposiums are given in universities on how it would have been impossible for Chamilly to spend time alone in a room with Mariana. History speaks to the contrary.

Before the threat, men had crossed the convent's inviolable threshold only once during Mariana's lifetime, in 1663, when her father had defended the city against the Spanish. Had Mariana's father been present in this month of August, the nuns would have turned to him, not to the French officers, for help. With Francisco and most of the dignitaries of Beja absent, the nuns had no choice but to summon Chamilly.

Word that Beja was in danger reached Francisco in Lisbon. Reinforcements arrived, sent from every corner of the country. The French soldiers were removed from the convent. Beja and the neighboring towns stood by, but nothing happened. The threat had been a ploy. While Portuguese troops assembled in the south, the Spanish traveled north. Four thousand horses and two thousand

Spanish musketeers raided Cabeça de Vide, Chamilly's old garrison town. The Portuguese army rushed north, but the Spanish had already pillaged and looted. Chamilly lost seventeen of his horses in the fight that ensued.[11]

Chamilly returned to Beja. The formal distance between the nuns and the officers was seemingly reinstated. Tea and pastries were served as always, yet the rules no longer applied. Now that he realized Mariana occupied her own house, did Chamilly's expectations change? The officer had glimpsed a world unforeseen and unimaginable. Events conspired in favor of love. The autumn campaign was postponed, and Chamilly and Mariana spent September and October of 1666 in each other's company. Unspoken promises lay between them.

AMIDST THE FLOURISH OF BULLFIGHTS, FIREWORKS, AND SPECTACLES, the royal newlyweds grew farther apart with every passing day.

One Sunday afternoon, October 17, 1666, the king, the queen, and Dom Pedro sat in a coach watching the Fidalgos practice Dom Afonso's favorite game. Called cane-play, the game mimicked combat using long reeds instead of spears. The king appointed eight leaders whose teams were to confront each other. Castelmelhor, cloaked in blue and gold, headed one of the squadrons. He faced the count of Marialva, one of Portugal's great generals, dressed in silver and nugget. Dom Pedro began praising Marialva. Taking offense, Dom Afonso hurled angry words toward his brother. Dom Pedro refused to recant. Drawing his dagger, Dom Afonso was about to strike when the queen, throwing herself between the two, begged for Dom Pedro's life. Dom Pedro, seizing the opportunity to distance himself from his brother, moved out of the palace that night.

Fearing the population might discover the rift between the two brothers, Castelmelhor tried to reconcile them, but to no avail. Marie-Françoise suggested to her husband that it would be wise to let her try. She had recently taken ill, probably in an attempt to shirk her conjugal duties. She now used her poor health to call on Dom Pedro to spend time at her bedside. The nineteen and twenty-year-old royals spent their evenings getting acquainted. The queen marked her appreciation for the handsome prince by sending her trusted servant to discreetly slide gifts beneath Dom Pedro's pillow. Every night, a trinket awaited him at his return. It is said his favorite was a garter laced with gold.

CIRCUMSTANCE NOW MADE MARIANA LESS AVAILABLE: AUTUMN marked the arrival of markets and fairs. The convent stocked up on salt and wine and cruppers and saddles for the mules. The nuns sold surpluses from their dairy farms and orchards as well as extra cases of marmalade and freshly-made pumpkin bread covered with almonds. The cellars needed to be filled with goods to last until the next summer and Mariana's responsibilities entailed keeping an exact account of all the provisions bought and sold.

November was also a month of notable religious festivities. The first of November was All Saints' Day, and the twentieth of the month marked the passing of the Infanta Isabel, the founder of Mariana's religious order in Portugal. The nuns were expected to devote more time to religious duties. Coupled with her administrative responsibilities, Mariana's days would have been extremely full.

The end of 1666 drew near. For the better part of that year, Chamilly had been stationed in Beja for weeks, sometimes months at a time. December 8 was the anniversary of Our Lady of Conception, the convent's patron saint. Every year, the convent gave a great banquet to mark the event and invited town dignitaries and visitors of note. This was the last public festivity before Christmas, after which the convent shut down completely. The holy period was private and strictly observed. After December 8, the nuns would not receive visitors until the new year, and Mariana would not see Chamilly for a month, if not more.

A few days before the banquet, the nuns were still preparing the food. Turtledoves, partridges, lapwings, plovers, and larks would be served along with ample platters of rice covered with dark beans. Vegetables and fruits provided color to the meal, and weeks were spent creating the exquisite paper cutouts that would serve to decorate the pastries.

The date drew closer. Long tables were set up. The nuns transformed the parlor into a sumptuous dining hall with tall candles for lights and rich tapestries covering the walls.

The French officers would have been invited to the yearly event. Chamilly had spent November at general headquarters preparing the January campaign. Nothing would have prevented him from returning to Beja for the occasion.

We can only guess at Mariana's impatience for Chamilly's return. According to code among the Portuguese, if a man looked into a woman's eyes, he silently asked to become her lover. If the woman met the gaze, it meant she acquiesced. Who can tell if such a look came to pass between Mariana and Chamilly. It would suffice for her to stand at the window of Mertola and for him to halt his horse a few feet away.

Memoirs of Marie-Françoise's Italian servant now kept in the British Museum tell the story of how, at the same time, miles away in Salvaterra, Dom Pedro, steadying his mount, stared upward toward the king's wife, sitting forlorn at a balcony. Marie-Françoise returned Dom Pedro's gaze. The queen and the young prince had fallen in love against every law in the land. Their affair, like Mariana and Chamilly's, would remain secret. Both came at a price. The fate of a kingdom and Mariana's life as she knew it lay in the balance.

The queen and the prince would emerge unscathed. They only had to bend the laws to suit their needs. Mariana and Chamilly would be subjected to a different reality, their desires subjugated to accommodate those of Marie-Françoise.

Did Chamilly and Mariana exchange looks, or was there a surreptitious whisper as plates were shuffled and wine was served? One thing is certain, sometime after the evening of December 8, 1666, as a "political alliance" formed between the queen and Dom Pedro, Mariana and Chamilly became lovers.

4

WHERE LOVERS MEET

"It is necessary to love like the Portuguese nun, with that ardent soul whose fiery mark is left for us in her letters."

STENDHAL, *ON LOVE* (1911)

"Never again will I see you in my room with all the ardor and exuberance you had me see?"

MARIANA ALCOFORADO, LETTER 4

HE CONVENT FORMED A RECTANGLE. THE SLEEPING quarters occupied the east and west areas and were divided into four sections. Fifty-six *little houses* were scattered throughout the gardens. They formed little clusters or stood alone. Mariana's house was probably part of a small compound built by her father for her and her sisters. Mariana belonged to a group that revered Saint John the Baptist, and the Alcoforado houses may have been situated in the garden that bore his name. The abbess locked the doors at night after matins and opened them again before dawn in time for morning prayers. Matins and vespers punctuated the course of the nuns' lives. The day started with sunrise and ended around one in the morning. The nuns were required to attend midnight matins and lauds in the main chapel. Chamilly would have to enter Mariana's room while the nuns sang the responsorial during matins.

The convent's occupancy was at its height, further complicating matters. Women slept crammed next to each other in the old dormitory, in one large room divided into fifty-six small cubicles built without ceilings and joined together, sometimes sleeping three in a cell only big enough for two. An extra thirty-eight cells and then fourteen more, built of dark wooden planks holding two beds each, had been added. Stone cupolas filled with blessed water were placed at the foot of each bed.

Mealtimes were oppressive. The women sat or stood side by side in a refectory too small for the growing number of nuns. The sisters, *sorore,* as the nuns of lower birth were called, sat separated from the mothers, *madres,* the appellation given to noblewomen. The rule of silence was applied, though seldom respected, and frequent bickering made any attempt at secrecy difficult. For Mariana and Chamilly to meet, it would be necessary to plan carefully. Night would be their only option.

The convent reopened after Christmas holidays. Hundreds of people, workers, priests, suppliers, and day laborers went to work, and the soldiers were invited back to the parlor. It would have been difficult for Mariana and Chamilly to communicate. Written messages were dangerous. Consequences were dire for anyone found acting as an intermediary. A man found passing letters between a nun and a man was condemned to four years of hard labor. A woman accused of the same crime was sentenced to seven years in Brazil. Mariana and Chamilly would have to converse in half sentences, underneath gusts of conversations, in a mixture of French, Portuguese, and Spanish.

Mariana's brother, Balthazar, was renowned for his jocular humor. During a burst of laughter, Mariana's handkerchief may have dropped to the floor. Hidden within the folds of the fabric, a note, a map, a time, and a way. Surreptitiously picked up by Chamilly, discreetly tucked into his sleeve, their hands may have touched furtively as the laced square of Irish linen was gallantly returned to its owner.

Chamilly would have to enter the house before Mariana's door was locked and leave in the morning after it was opened. Mariana probably turned to her mother's servant for help. Bastiana, a mulatto, had been with Mariana's family for as long as Mariana had been alive. Given to Mariana at the death of her mother, probably to help care for Perigrina, Bastiana was the child of an African slave and her owner. These children were often freed and became servants.

Chamilly would need to tread quietly along darkened archways to the sound of the nuns singing back and forth to each other. Candles lining the chapel walls sent a flickering light through the inner courtyard, and the moon drew strange shadows against the sculptures of saints, creating odd reminders of the women who populated the walkways. At the end of the southeastern archway, a beautifully ornate wooden door cut directly into the ceramic. The door opened onto the garden of Saint John the Baptist, where the nun's houses hid behind holly oaks, cork oaks, flowers, and plantings.

Mariana's little sister was seven now, and she would have shared Mariana's quarters, though it is possible she and Bastiana shared the house Francisco had built for Catarina, the sister who had passed away. Perhaps Mariana entrusted Perigrina to her friend and confidante, Dona Brites. Four Dona Brites lived at the convent at the time Mariana knew Chamilly. Her friend was probably the youngest of the four. The answer may be simpler. Bastiana would have put the child to bed, as she must have every night, while the nuns were at matins. Chamilly would have quietly walked by the child's bed, leaving Perigrina to sleep undisturbed.

Elaborately sculpted beds, made of massive oak, decorated the nuns' bedrooms. Rugs from India or Persia lay on the floors. Massive armoires held their dresses, and draperies and woven tapestries decorated the walls.

At twenty-six, Mariana had lodgings of her own, a profession, a name, and a voice within her community. She had servants. She created income. She held the right to vote on matters that concerned her directly. She conversed expertly on subjects forbidden to most women and her opinions were held in high esteem by men of power. But for all her worldliness, Mariana's cloistered existence did not prepare her for the feelings that must have submerged her, as clothing gave way to flesh.

The letters confess to Chamilly's skills as a lover in every sentence. The young captain had served under a famous libertine and fellow Burgundian, Roger Bussy-Rabutin, who handled irony as skillfully as he did the sword. Between battles and bedmates, Rabutin had written a book on the dissolute games the French played at court. Under his aegis, it is quite possible the young Chamilly learned the art of some war and much love.

The Franciscan order to which Mariana belonged did not allow portraits or any likeness of oneself. Her image is unknown to us, but we know enough to conjure up a young woman at the height of her powers. She would not have worn rouge or powder. Her hair, cut short since the age of sixteen, would have lent a boyish air to her appearance. The long black veil worn by the nuns fell below her shoulders, nearing her waist. Beneath it, a white cloth wrapped around her head and neck and again, under this, a silver chain or row of precious stones, a dress, and then some lace. Chamilly would never experience the thrill of the forbidden in quite the same way again, whispers soothing and guiding the lovers through the darkness of the night.

Unsuspected and unseen, Chamilly and Mariana entered a world more intimate than a prayer and more ethereal than air. Perhaps only a game at first, Mariana would teach the soldier a different kind of love from which neither would ever fully recover. Their meeting would transform them both.

Portuguese scholars believe Chamilly left with the morning sun, disguised as painters clothing. The convent was constantly under repair and the presence of a laborer in the early hours of the day would not be questioned. Documents describe how lovers like Chamilly cloaked themselves in painters' capes, wearing large hats in order to enter and exit convents at will.

Chamilly and Mariana probably saw each other sporadically through January and February of 1667. The troops spent time between headquarters and their garrisons. Schomberg kept mounting expeditions that were constantly cancelled. Dom Afonso's acts of cruelty toward Marie-Françoise were becoming public knowledge. The king now openly shunned the queen, flaunting his mistresses for all to see, roaming the street at night, keeping lewd company, and spoiling for fights. Outraged by the king's treatment of the beautiful Marie-Françoise, the Fidalgos began rallying around their queen. Despite several entreaties by Marie-Françoise's entourage, Schomberg, officially under the employ of King Afonso, refused to get involved.

UNABLE TO GET CASTELMELHOR TO FOCUS ON MILITARY AFFAIRS, Schomberg decided to launch a campaign on his own. Chamilly and Balthazar were called at the end of February and departed on March 7 or 8 to take out a regiment of Castilian cavalry, an Irish infantry, and four companies of Catalonians situated in the town of Albuquerque on the Spanish border.

The men walked through the night, crossing two small rivers with water up to their midriffs. They arrived soaking wet at the outskirts of the town an hour before daybreak and began placing ladders to scale the walls. The door to the lower town gave way. Fighting began in its narrow streets. Horses toppled, crushing soldiers and town folk. Soldiers resorted to hand-to-hand combat. The Irish infantry, working for the Spanish, stacked the walls with hay and started a fire.

By midday, Schomberg's men were fighting unprotected in the streets. They started to fall. Schomberg sent out orders for his infantry to retire. A bullet hit the captain responsible for the foot soldiers, killing him instantaneously. Ordering the lower town pillaged, Schomberg called a retreat.

Chamilly pulled away the injured from the bloodied streets and laid them into carts and over the backs of tired horses. The captain killed had been a friend. In the aftermath of his first failed battle, Chamilly may well have yearned for the sanctuary of Mariana's house.

Horses' hooves pounded Beja's streets and alcohol flowed, dulling the pain, while the wounded overtook the city. War, unrelenting, broke down barriers once again as soldiers, nuns, and the general population came together to tend the wounded and bury the dead.

A few weeks later, France and Portugal signed a ten-year treaty, ratified on March 31, 1667, in an effort by Louis XIV to keep the war alive and prevent the English from brokering a peace agreement. Louis XIV instructed Schomberg to finish depleting the weakened Spanish forces, but Castelmelhor forbade Schomberg from undertaking any substantial expeditions. In the months of April and May, when a light cool breeze normally sent soldiers into the grueling hardships of battle, orders were given to remain idle. While politics wreaked havoc on plans of war, the French officer and the nun kept time at bay inventing a world of their own in the darkened nights of the fragrant Portuguese spring. For the few nuns who noticed Mariana's transformation from girl to woman, they would presume she had entered a state they called the *Muda*.

The *Muda* was a retreat from the daily practice of life and religious duties. Considered a form of mysticism, this time period could last weeks or even months. Sometimes involving fasting, often self-flagellation, the nuns described the experience as entering an altered state akin to ecstasy, or as if they were experiencing love incarnate. They talked of burning sensations, of the flesh being relieved, and it is difficult not to equate their descriptions to a form of sexual release. More than a simple retreat, the *Muda* transported the women onto another spiritual plane, cleansing and reinvigorating their faith. *Muda*s took place at different times in the nuns' lives. A nun was only required to eat communally at the refectory one hundred and fifty times a year, and nuns saved up their days in anticipation of entering a *Muda*. During the spring and summer of 1667, when Chamilly was available, it is possible Mariana sent Perigrina to live with Dona Brites and stopped attending meals. If Mariana did invoke the *Muda* to justify her absence, she would not have been that far from telling the truth.

SCHOMBERG, IN AN EFFORT TO KEEP THE MEN OCCUPIED, ORGAnized runs into enemy territory. Attacking unguarded villages, robbing the occupants of their silver, jewelry, and sometimes furniture, the officers kept accumulating riches. The Spanish returned the favor and Chamilly was among those sent to rescue unguarded Portuguese villages.

The runs were not enough. Bored, the soldiers started carousing in the streets, disturbing the peace, harassing the local populations, and cavorting with local girls. The actions of the foreign soldiers further alienated the Alcoforado brothers, Balthazar and Miguel. The younger Alcoforado was among those who believed that Portugal had no need of foreigners telling them how to conduct a war. Balthazar welcomed the French, and his friendship with Chamilly must have proved irksome to Miguel. Certainly the mounting disturbances in June of 1667 prompted Miguel to write to Dom Pedro asking him to remove the French soldiers from Beja.[1] Dom Pedro agreed, but this did not suit Schomberg's hope of convincing Castelmelhor to attack the Spanish, and so Dom Pedro's orders were ignored. The soldiers remained garrisoned in Beja, but the officers were no longer perceived as the heroes they once were.

The implacable heat of summer interrupted the runs into enemy territory. Hunts and gambling replaced battles. Surrogates for war, the hunts helped build an esprit de corps. The more the men cared for each other, the harder they fought, the better they knew each other, the more effective they became out on the battlefield. Briquemault knew his men intimately, and he was sensitive to their slightest changes in moods or demeanor. Briquemault would be quick to notice any behavior out of the ordinary coming from his favorite officer. Chamilly's official relationship with Mariana was certainly known, possibly even encouraged. Relationships between nuns and officers further helped keep his men in check. However, with weeks of inactivity stretching into months, and with tensions mounting on all sides, any inkling of impropriety would call for Briquemault to take matters into his own hands.

The summer months of 1667 would be the longest un-interrupted time the lovers would know.

SOMETIME DURING THE SECOND WEEK IN AUGUST, MARIE-Françoise wrote to Schomberg asking him to assess the army's position toward her and Dom Pedro. The response was delivered as she was preparing for bed on a Saturday around midnight. The news was not good. Schomberg felt that part of the army would support the king. Dawn was breaking when she finally fell asleep, the missive still in her hand.

Awakened by her servants, in haste, she joined the king for mass. She arrived as he was departing. A new mass was ordered especially for her. Remembering Schomberg's letter and fearing it might be discovered, she sent her confessor to fetch it. But he found the king in her chamber talking with Castelmelhor's mother, the queen's lady-in-waiting. Desperate to create a diversion and avert disaster, Marie-Françoise collapsed into her confessor's arms. Carried by a half-dozen servants, the queen entered her room to find the king lying on her bed. Dom Afonso, frightened by the spectacle of the unconscious queen, leapt upward and ordered the bed made. The queen, coughing and instantly resuscitated, begged to be put onto the unmade bed. Her fumbling hands found the letters tangled in her nightgown. Dom Afonso had not bothered to move it.

Marie-Françoise finally enjoyed good fortune on August 21. That day, Castelmelhor was away and his replacement, the secretary of state, who normally saw very little of the queen, presented her with a letter from the kingdom of Angola. Seizing the opportunity, the queen plunged into a long list of complaints. She was kept away from matters of state, her dowry was still not paid in full, the troops' salaries were missing, the religious houses and charitable asylums were underfunded, and even noblemen were robbed of their pensions while Castelmelhor's friends wallowed in riches. The discussion began to escalate.

Incapable of holding back any longer, the old loyal secretary started shouting at her in Portuguese: "You have no reason to complain of the Portuguese, Madame."

"I do not complain of the Portuguese, it is but of three or four that I complain," she retorted, ordering the old man to be silent. He shouted louder, ranting he wanted the world to hear him. The queen rose to leave. The secretary seized the hem of her gown. She snatched her dress out of his hand. Making her way through a sea of stunned and silent courtiers, she stormed away. War at court had begun.

The ensuing confusion further delayed payments of soldiers' wages. Frustrated, the soldiers took to helping themselves to goods in local stalls, loitering, accosting women of rank, and spoiling for fights. Unable to control the mayhem, the French officers were losing the trust of the people. The citizens kept complaining, asking that the soldiers be removed.

Castelmelhor returned to Lisbon to find his position heavily compromised. Told to be suspicious of Schomberg, Castelmelhor ordered the general to the Alentejo. September 1, standing in a deserted audience chamber looking out on the river as the sun was setting, a servant discreetly informed Castelmelhor that an attempt on his life, organized by Dom Pedro, was to take place during the night. Frightened, realizing his suspicions of Schomberg had been orchestrated by enemies of the king, Castelmelhor ordered the guards to the palace thereby thwarting the attempt on his life. Reversing course, Dom Pedro now accused Castelmelhor of wanting to kill him, demanding that Castelmelhor be fired. The king having refused, Castelmelhor now ordered Schomberg back to Lisbon with the army.

By now Schomberg had received orders from Turenne telling him to side with Dom Pedro. Hindering Castelmelhor's orders, Schomberg dispersed his troops, sending his men to do runs along the Spanish border. Retaliating, Castelmelhor confined the army to the Alentejo and recalled the entire Portuguese fleet into Lisbon's harbor. Civil war was brewing.

Pressure mounted on all sides. Dom Pedro rallied around him the counselors of state, the Council of Twenty-four and the Fidalgos. Castelmelhor begged the queen to intercede on his behalf, unaware that by now Marie-Françoise and Dom Pedro were "allies." Instead, Marie-Françoise forced the king to relieve Castelmelhor of his duties. By September 13, Castelmelhor hid nearby at a friend's house, governing through the old secretary who had rebuked the queen.

Once again, the king called the army to his side, but Schomberg, keeping his men as far away from Lisbon as possible, now directed his troops to the small castle of Ferreyra, held by the Spanish, cleaning up the borders along the way, taking prisoners and burning a few villages. The end of September drew near.

Dom Pedro entered the palace on October 5 with the intention of deposing the king. Upon seeing his brother, Dom Afonso shouted, "Bring me my sword."

"Here is mine, sire, for you to use against me or to defend you with."

Dom Pedro, looking through the window, realized the king was protected by the army bivouacking below in the courtyard.

Marie-Françoise arrived. "What brings you here?" said the king.

"I am here to help you," said Marie-Françoise.

"I rather think you came to see my brother," said Dom Afonso.

A crowd gathered below. Seizing the opportunity, the old secretary of state pushed the queen, the king, and Dom Pedro onto the balcony. All three raised their hands in unison.

The crowd shouted, "Viva, viva the king." Dom Pedro, realizing he could not take over then, insisted the king fire the old secretary of state. Dom Afonso responded by taking out his flute and playing as he walked through the crowd of Fidalgos, offering his pardon to those he encountered. That night, sensing all was lost, a disguised Castelmelhor rode off to his estate a hundred and twenty miles away. The king was now completely isolated.

Throughout the month of October, a campaign vilifying Dom Afonso was launched. Afonso's impotence was made public. Newspapers filled with articles ridiculing the king were printed on large sheets of paper and circulated throughout the country, turning the population against him. At the same time, Dom Pedro kept gaining favor by granting wishes and donating money to charitable causes. Aware that the king could still call on the army, Schomberg sent the soldiers back to their respective quarters, making it impossible for Dom Afonso to rely on military help.

Chamilly returned to Beja, but access to Mariana was difficult. Tensions between the French officers and the population escalated.

A month and a half later, the queen fled to the Franciscan convent of Esperança on a Monday and sent the following letter to her husband,

To my King and Lord.—I left my country, I sold my fortune to seek Your Majesty, and to love you and serve you—Your Majesty is not satisfied with me, I am forced to return to my own country for justice. Your Majesty must allow me, and in justice must give me my dowry, and give me license to go hence, in duty bound to grant this grace to me a stranger.

Lisbon, November 18, 1667.

The departure was calculated to attract sympathy from the population and drive Dom Afonso mad. Roused into a monstrous rage, Afonso made his way to the convent. Thundering at the door, he demanded to see his wife. The trembling gatekeeper brought the mother superior to the gate.

"Open this door," commanded the king.

"I cannot, sire, Her Majesty has taken the keys," the gatekeeper replied.

"Fetch me an axe! Fetch me the carpenters and locksmith!" roared the king. A crowd gathered. Dom Pedro stood watching the spectacle before rushing to Dom Afonso's side. Dom Pedro spoke at the top of his voice so that all would hear him advise the king to return to the palace and let the council decide.

Dom Afonso attempted to escape from the palace to join his army, but his plans were discovered and thwarted. Dom Pedro declared, "If the king brings the army back to Lisbon, the Spanish will follow. For the safety of the state, he must be stopped."

The whole country was at a standstill. Chamilly and his companions, still in Beja, awaited orders.

On November 23, 1667, Dom Pedro locked Dom Afonso in his rooms. Tortured into abdicating, Dom Afonso signed a document "of his own free will" proclaiming Dom Pedro as Prince Regent. A hundred miles away, Castelmelhor fled by foot, walking at night, until he reached the border. The reign of King Dom Afonso VI was over. A new regime was about to take hold, and for Marie-Françoise to be part of it, she needed to be perceived as an unfortunate victim.

Ships stood by to return Marie-Françoise to France while secret plans were underway for her to remain, annul her marriage, and marry Dom Pedro. She needed public opinion on her side. The population, volatile and angered at the foreign soldiers, endangered the queen's designs. It was imperative that French officers take control of the unruly soldiers responsible for abuses around the country, and that they prevent any transgressions capable of igniting an already incendiary situation.

A document drawn in Chamilly's name, guaranteeing him a safe passage back to France, arrived sometime during this period. The document grants Chamilly permission to leave at any time without facing desertion charges. It also reinstates Chamilly into the French army with his advancement intact. The document, personally signed by Louis XIV, raises interesting questions. On the brink of a civil war, when all of Schomberg's ablest men were needed, it is strange Chamilly was given permission to leave.

Chamilly's older brother, Herard, is probably the one responsible for the document being issued. Warned by Briquemault of his younger brother's potential indiscretion, Herard had a vested interest in insuring that Chamilly leave Portugal with his reputation intact.[2]

Herard had returned from exile determined to regild the family name and return it to its former glory. He had married a wealthy merchant's daughter to replenish his empty coffers and the Great Condé had named him governor of the castle of Dijon in his home province of Burgundy. Greatly admired for his tactical intelligence and diplomatic skills, Burgundian nobility had elected him as their representative (1665–1677). The Great Condé considered him one of his most trusted advisers and according to the historian Eugène Beauvois, Herard was greatly admired by Louis XIV. News from Briquemault probably reached Herard as he was busy preparing the first phases of a surprise attack for Louis XIV on the Spanish territory of Franche-Comté.

Franche-Comté abutted the territory of Burgundy and Louis XIV considered this attack a warm-up battle on his way to claim parts of the Netherlands promised to him in his wife's unpaid dowry. Herard's diplomatic and tactical skills, crucial to the gathering of intelligence and plotting of the attack, ideally positioned him for asking King Louis XIV to sign a document guaranteeing Chamilly a safe passage to France. Franche-Comté was the perfect excuse and motivator for bringing Chamilly home. No one need know the true reasons behind Chamilly's return.

Cause enough would compel Briquemault, a family friend, to turn to Herard for help. The longer Chamilly spent time in Beja, the more exposed he became. Schomberg's orders to keep the officers in Beja only added to the danger of Chamilly's affair with Mariana becoming public. Miguel's open dislike of the French soldiers may also have hinted at his distrust of Mariana's friendship with Chamilly, and Briquemault knew that Miguel would not hesitate to use the scandal to banish the French from Portugal.

An affair with a nun, objectionable but somewhat accepted under normal circumstances (a man faced only two months in prison or a fine), became unacceptable if conducted with a French officer. That the nun was the daughter of the rich and powerful Francisco da Costa Alcoforado only made matters worse. At this time of tumultuous civil unrest, the scandal resulting from the affair being discovered would carry dangerous consequences for the safety of the nation, and the reputation of France. Knowledge that Chamilly had violated Mariana would be enough to transform the citizens of the town into a mob. Portuguese officers resentful of Schomberg's successes would seize the opportunity to undermine his command. Marie-Françoise herself would not be immune to the scandal, and the public outrage would jeopardize her plans to depose the king. In France, the Chamilly name would become inexorably tarnished.

The document offered a discreet solution. Issued without any date other than the year 1667, it allowed Chamilly to leave at any time. War records place Chamilly at the Portuguese battle of Ferreyra at the end of September 1667, and he is next mentioned arriving in Dijon, France, on February 9 of the following year. Briquemault's decision to have Chamilly leave, and a letter from Herard asking Chamilly to join him, must have coincided sometime at the beginning of October. Portuguese outrage was at its peak and plans for Franche-Comté were firming up. This possibility is further confirmed when we know that Herard spent October in Paris on official business with the king while at the same time secretly plotting the attack. Depending on the weather, Chamilly's voyage would take anywhere from four days to two months.

By November, finding a ship had become difficult. The king was deposed. Lisbon was at a standstill. The port was in turmoil. The entire Portuguese fleet crowded the docks. French ships were not leaving, waiting for the outcome of Marie-Françoise's discussions with the court of Portugal. Chamilly would have to travel along the southern coast of Portugal because Lisbon, the normal departure point for French soldiers, was impracticable. The southern route held the added advantage of landing Chamilly in Marseille, much closer geographically to his brother's castle.[3]

Unaware of the political undercurrents that were pushing Chamilly away from her, Mariana did not understand Chamilly's reasons for leaving. Having spent her life assaulted by war, the present state of affairs was simply part of a long litany of woes. There were no signs that war was relenting. The treaty signed a few months earlier between the French and the Portuguese stipulated that French soldiers remain in Portugal for another ten years. With the country up in arms, every officer was needed. And then, other officers had fallen in love, and many were choosing to marry daughters of noblemen anxious to find a good party for their daughters. The population, finally swayed in the queen's direction, now begged her to stay and marry Dom Pedro. The whole country favored the queen's love for her brother-in-law, over the loyalty she owed her husband, the king. Mariana came from a world where love took precedence over all things. How could she understand Chamilly's decision to leave? Did she know that a long time ago Chamilly the youth had chosen his country over his family? Called to serve his king, Chamilly the soldier now chose duty over love.

Warned by Balthazar and by a note from Chamilly's alluding to his departure, not knowing or fully understanding the reasons forcing Chamilly to leave, Mariana would never know why she had been sacrificed.

The day he left, Mariana faced the rest of her life. From now onward, she would tread through corridors leading to chapels emptied of their meaning. Her little house no longer a refuge, only a reminder. And so, in the darkness of her room, Mariana Alcoforado, a twenty-seven-year-old nun, buried in the confines of a convent located in one of the most remote provinces in Portugal, exerted control over her pain in the only way she knew how. She began to write.

The Letters

I

(Mariana's first letter is written while Chamilly is still in Beja,
preparing to leave.) circa November–December 1667

Love, consider well your lack of foresight. Ah!
Unfortunate love! You were betrayed and you betrayed me
with false expectations. A passion that held such sweet
promise now brings a mortal despair more cruel than the
absence that provokes it.

Ho! This absence for which my pain, ingenious as it is,
can not find a name bleak enough, will thus deprive me forever of looking at those eyes wherein I saw such love, eyes
that filled me with ecstasy, that were all manner of things
and were for me enough? Alas, mine are deprived of the
only light that made them sparkle; all they have left are tears
and they do nothing but cry relentlessly since I learnt you[1]
were finally resolved to leave, a parting so unbearable it will
surely hasten my death.

Yet I find myself rather attached to the unhappiness caused
by you alone. My life was yours from when first I saw you
and I take some pleasure in sacrificing it to you. A thousand
times a day I send my every sigh to find you. They seek you

out in every place but their reward for all this worry is but too sincere a warning brought on by my misfortune that cruelly forbids me to flatter myself and that tells me at all times; Cease, cease, unfortunate Mariana, to be consumed in vain, and to look for a lover you will never see; he crossed the ocean to flee from you, he is in France surrounded by life's pleasures, he thinks nothing of your pain. He dismisses and exempts you from fits of passion for which he is not grateful.

But no, I cannot bring myself to judge you so harshly. I want too much to excuse you. I do not want to believe you have forgotten me. Am I not miserable enough without tormenting myself with false suspicions? And why should I try and forget all the cares you took to show me your love? I was so charmed by your attentions that I would be ungrateful if I did not love you with the same excesses my passion gave me when you would grant me yours. How can it be that the memories of such pleasurable moments have become so cruel? And why must they, against their very nature now serve to tyrannize my heart?

Alas! Your last letter reduced it to a peculiar state: its pounding was so extreme it made, so it seemed, efforts to leave my body and go find you; I was so overcome by all these violent emotions that I remained abandoned by my senses for more than three hours; I stopped myself from returning to a life I must lose since I cannot keep it for you; at last, despite myself, I saw light. I flattered myself thinking I was dying of love; besides I felt relief, believing I would no longer have to witness my heart being ripped apart by the pain of your absence.

Following these events I suffered various indispositions; but can I ever be without ills if I do not see you? Nonetheless, I suffer them in silence for they come from you. How can this be? Is this my reward for loving you so tenderly? What does it matter, I am resolved to worship you all my life, and to see no other, and I can assure you that you would do well to do the same. Could you be satisfied with a passion less ardent than mine? It may be you will find greater beauty (though you once told me I was somewhat beautiful) but never will you find such love and all the rest is nothing. No longer fill your letters with useless things and no longer write I should remember you. I cannot forget you, nor forget you gave me hope you would come and spend some time with me. Alas, why not all your life?

Were it possible for me to leave this miserable cloister I would not await the outcome of your promises in Portugal. Without measure or precaution, I would go and find you, follow you and love you through all the world. I dare not think this possible. I dare not feed a hope that would surely give me some pleasure and I want only to be sensitive to pain.

Still I must confess. The opportunity my brother gives me to write has caused me some unexpected joy and has suspended for a time the agony I am in. I beseech you to tell me why you were so determined to charm me as you did, when you knew well you must abandon me. And why were you so bent on making me unhappy? Would that you had left me in peace in my cloister! Had I committed against you some injustice? Forgive me, I do not blame you. I am in no state to think of vengeance and I blame only the harshness of my fate. I find that in separating us, fate wronged us more than we could fear; it will not know how to separate our hearts, love which is more powerful has bound them together for all of our life! Should mine still hold some interest write to me often. I well deserve you take some care to send me news of your heart and of your circumstances; but mostly come and see me.

Adieu. I cannot leave this page, it will fall into your hands, would that I had the same good fortune. Alas! fool that I am, this cannot be. Adieu, I can bear no more. Adieu, love me always and make me suffer even greater woes.

I I

Your lieutenant tells me at present that a storm has forced
you to moor in the kingdom of the Algarve. I fear you may
have suffered much at sea, and this apprehension has
occupied me so that I have quit thinking of my pains. Are
you quite sure your lieutenant takes greater care than I in all
that happens to you? Why is he better informed and finally
why have you not written to me!

I am most sad if you found no occasion since your departure, and even more so if one was found and you did not
seize it; the injustice you do me and your ingratitude are extreme: but I would despair if they brought you some misfortune, and I much rather they remain unpunished than if I
were avenged. I resist all appearances that should persuade
me that you do not love me, and I feel much more inclined
to blindly give way to my passion than to the reasons you
give me to complain of your lack of care. How you would
have spared me worries, had your ways been as languishing
the first days I saw you as they have seemed to me of late!
But who would not have been deceived, as I, by so many attentions and to whom would they not have seemed sincere?
How difficult it is to bring oneself to question at length the
good faith of our loved ones!

I can see that the poorest excuse suits you, and without your taking care to make any, the love I have for you serves you so faithfully I consent to find you guilty only so that I may delight in the pleasure of defending you myself.

I was consumed by your assiduities, your exuberance inflamed me, your kindness fascinated me, you won me with your vows, I was seduced by my own violent inclination, and what follows such sweet and joyful beginnings are but tears, and sighs, and a grievous death for which I find no remedy. It is true I found surprising pleasures in loving you, but they cost me strange sufferings and all the stirrings that you cause me are extreme.

Had I stubbornly resisted your love, had I caused you to feel dejection or jealousy to inflame you further, had you noticed some careful artifice in my conduct, had I at last wanted to oppose my reason to the natural inclination I have for you, which you quickly pointed out to me (though my efforts would have most certainly been in vain), you could punish me severely and make use of your power. But you appeared loving before telling me you loved me; you protested a great passion, I was charmed, and I succumbed to loving you passionately. You were not blinded as I was. How then could you suffer my being driven to this state.

What use could you make of my fits of passion that could only irk you? You knew you would not be forever in Portugal, why then have chosen me to render so unhappy? You would have found, no doubt, in this country, some woman more beautiful, with whom you would have shared as many pleasures, since you sought only coarse ones. She would have loved you faithfully for as long as she saw you. Time would have cured her of your absence, and you could have left her without deceit or cruelty. Your behavior is more that of a tyrant, fond of persecution, than that of a lover who must think only of pleasing. Alas! Why do you inflict such rigors on a heart that is yours. I see well how easy it is for you to let yourself be turned against me as it was for me to let myself be convinced in your favor. I would have resisted greater reasons than those that forced you to leave me, without having to use all my love or without thinking I was doing some extraordinary thing. Any reason would have seemed weak and none could have torn me away from you; but you wanted to take advantage of the pretexts you found for returning to France; a ship was leaving; why not let it leave? Your family had written; do you not know all the persecutions inflicted by my own? Your honour begged you to forsake me; did I have any care of mine? You were obliged to go and serve your king; if all that is said of him is true, he does not need your help and he would have excused you.

I would have been too happy had we spent our lives together, but since a cruel absence separates us, it seems that I must be content with not being unfaithful and I would not, for all the world, commit so dark a deed.

What! You knew the depth of my love and of my tenderness and still you could resolve to leave me and forever expose me to the fear that I am bound to have thinking you will remember me only to sacrifice me to some new passion? I can see that I love you like a mad woman; but I do not complain of the violent movements of my heart, I am getting accustomed to its persecutions and I could not live without the joy I am discovering of loving you amidst a thousand sorrows: I am forever persecuted with extreme annoyance by a hatred and disgust for all things; my family, my friends, this convent are insufferable to me; all I am required to see and all my obligations seem odious to me. I am so fond of my passion that it seems that all my actions and all my duties have only to do with you. Yes, I feel guilty if every moment is not yours. Alas! What would I do without such hate and such love to fill my heart? Could I survive not being incessantly consumed, and lead a life tranquil and languid? This emptiness and insensitivity is not for me.

Everyone has noticed the entire change in my humor, in my manners and in myself, Mother Superior has spoken of it to me sharply at first and then with some kindness; I do not know what it is I answered her, it seems I confessed everything to her. The strictest nuns have pity on my state, it even provides them with some consideration and some care for me. Everyone is touched by my love, while you remain in a state of profound indifference, writing me only icy letters, full of repetitions—half the paper is empty, and I can see that you are dying to have them finished.

Dona Brites harassed me these last few days to make me leave my room and thinking she would distract me, she took me strolling on the balcony from which we can see Mertola;[2] I followed her, and was immediately struck by a cruel memory that made me cry the rest of the day; she brought me back, and I threw myself on my bed where I thought a thousand times on the little hope I see of ever recovering. What they do to allay me sours my pain. I find in the remedies themselves further reasons to afflict me.

I saw you often pass in these domains with an air that would charm me, and I was on this balcony that fatal day I started to perceive the first effects of my unfortunate passion. It seemed to me you wanted to charm me and though you did not know me, I persuaded myself that you had noticed me amidst all those that were with me. I imagined that when you halted you were quite happy to allow me to see you better so that I might admire your skill and good graces when riding your horse. A sense of fright took me by surprise when you made it pass a difficult tract, I was secretly interested in all your actions. I felt quite sure you were not indifferent to me, and I took for me all that you did. You know all too well what followed these beginnings and though I have nothing to hide, I must not write of this for fear of making you more guilty, if this is possible, and then to have to chide myself for making so many useless efforts to compel you to be faithful.

You will not be. Can I hope that my letters and my chiding will succeed to touch on your ingratitude when my love and indulgence failed? I hold too many proofs to the contrary, your unjust ways leave me no reason to doubt, and I must fear the worst, since you have abandoned me. Will your charms win only myself? Will no other eyes find you pleasing? I think I would not be angry if affections found in others could, in some way, justify my own, and I would like that all the women of France found you charming, that none be charmed, and that none please you.

This design is useless and impossible and I have sufficiently experienced your lack of character to know that you will forget me without any help or without need for a new passion.

Maybe I want you to have some reasonable excuse? It is true that I would be more unhappy, but you would be less guilty. I can see that you will remain in France without need for great pleasures and of your own free will; Does the fatigue of a long voyage, some semblance of propriety, the fear you may not return my passion keep you? Ah! do not fear me. I will be content with seeing you from time to time and knowing simply that you and I are in one place. Maybe I flatter myself, and you will be more touched by the rejection and the severity of another than you were by my favors. Is it possible that harsh treatment will inflame you?

But before engaging in a great passion, think well on the excess of my pain, on the uncertainty of my plans, on the turmoil in my heart, on the extravagance of my letters, on my trustfulness, on my despair, on my wishes, on my jealousy. Ah! You will render yourself miserable. I implore you, take heed, so that at least what I suffer may serve you in some way.

Five or six months ago you entrusted in me a woeful secret and you acknowledged all too candidly that you had loved another woman in your country. If she prevents you from returning, tell me without sparing so that I may cease to languish. Some fragment of hope sustains me still, and I would be relieved (should it have no tomorrow) to lose it truly and lose myself as well; send me her portrait with a few of her letters, and write me all that she tells you. Maybe I will find reasons to console myself or to afflict me greater. I cannot remain long in my present state, there is no change that would not be favorable. I would also like the portrait of your brother and of your sister-in-law; all that means something to you is to me most precious and I am entirely devoted to everything that touches you. I am left with nothing of myself. There are moments when it seems I could even serve the one you love. Your bad treatment and your disdain have broken me so thoroughly that I dare not even believe it possible to think I could be jealous and yet not displease you, and I believe I do the greatest harm in the world to fault you. I am often convinced that I should not let you see with such fury, as I do, feelings you disavow.

An officer has long been waiting for your letter, I was determined to write it in such a fashion so that you may receive it without aversion, but it is too extravagant, it must be finished. Alas: It is not within my power to bring myself to do this, it seems to me I speak to you when I write, and that you are more present. The next one will not be as long or as troublesome, you will be able to open and read it with this assurance; it is true, I must not speak of a passion which displeases you, and I will speak of it no more.

It will be a year in a few days since I gave myself to you without reserve, your passion seemed to me very ardent and sincere and I never would have thought that my favors would so annoy you as to force you to travel five hundred leagues and that you would rather encounter shipwrecks only to flee from me; I did not deserve such treatment. You can remember my modesty, my shame, and my confusion, but you do not remember what made you love me in spite of yourself.

The officer who will bring you this letter reminds me for the fourth time that he must leave. How he is pressing. He is abandoning no doubt some other unfortunate woman in this country.

Adieu, I have more difficulty in finishing my letter than you had in leaving me, possibly forever. Adieu, I dare not whisper a thousand tender names, or abandon myself freely to my wayward passion. I love you a thousand times more than my life, and a thousand times more than I can think. How you are dear to me and how you are cruel! You do not write, I could not stop myself from telling you this as well; I will start again and the officer will leave; what of it if he leaves? I write more for myself than for you, I try only to soothe myself, it is as well, the length of my letter will scare you and you will not read it. What have I done to be so miserable? And why have you poisoned my life? Would that I was born in some other country! Adieu, Forgive me! I no longer dare ask you to love me; see to what extent fate has reduced me! Adieu.

III

(circa January or February 1668)

What will become of me and what do you want me to do? I find myself quite estranged from all I had imagined; I had hoped you would write to me from wherever you went and that your letters would be exceedingly long; that you would sustain my passion with hopes of seeing you again, that an absolute trust in your loyalty would provide me with some rest; and that I would remain all the same in a tolerable state without extreme afflictions; I had even contrived a few feeble plots to make, as much I could, able efforts to cure myself, if only I knew with certainty you had well forgotten me. Your absence, the distance between us, some stirrings of devotion, the fear of ruining entirely the rest of my health through so many sleepless nights and so many worries, the little hope of your ever returning, the coldness of your passion and of your last good-byes, your departure founded on such weak excuses, and a thousand other reasons, that are only too good, and too useless, seemed to promise me some help, if it became necessary. Having only myself to struggle with, I could not trust my weaknesses, nor apprehend all I suffer to-day. Alas! How I deserve to be pitied for not sharing my sorrows with you, and for being the only one with pain. This thought kills me and I die of fright thinking you may have never been sentient to all our pleasures.

Yes, I now perceive the ill faith of all your actions: you betrayed me every time you said you were thrilled to be alone with me. I owe your attentiveness and loving transports only to my importunities. In cold blood you made the design to inflame me, you saw my passion only as a conquest and your heart was never deeply touched. Are you not very unhappy and do you possess so little grace that you knew only to employ my emotions thus? And how can it be that with such love I could not make you truly happy? I regret out of love for you, the infinite pleasures you have lost; can it be that you did not want to relish them. Ah! To know them, you would doubtless find that they are more delicate than the pleasure of deceit and you would have discovered that we are far happier, and that we feel something far more touching, when we love violently, than when we are loved.

I do not know who I am, what I do, or what I desire; I am torn by a thousand contrary emotions. Can one imagine so deplorable a state? I love you to distraction, and I care for you enough, not to dare, perhaps, wish upon you the same torments; I would kill myself, or I would die of grief without the need to kill myself, were I told you know no rest, that your life is filled with turmoil and confusion, that you cry endlessly, and that everything is odious to you. I can barely tend my ills. How could I endure a pain born out of yours, would it not be for me a thousand times more harrowing?

Yet, I cannot resign myself to wish that you think of me no more; and to speak sincerely, I am furiously jealous of all

that brings you joy, and of what touches your heart and
your taste in France. I do not know why I write to you.
I can see that you will only pity me and I do not want
your pity.

I am so angry at myself when I think of all I sacrificed for
you: I have lost my reputation, I exposed myself to my
family's fury, to the severity of this country's laws against
nuns, moreover to your ingratitude, which seems to me to
be the greatest of my woes. And yet, I can see that my
remorse is not real, that in earnest, I would have liked, for
love of you, to have encountered greater dangers, and that I
take a morbid pleasure in having risked my life and honor
for you. All I hold most precious, should it not have been
at your disposal? And should I not be satisfied for having
employed it thus? It even seems to me that I am not happy
with my pains or the excess of my love, even if I cannot,
Alas! flatter myself enough to be pleased with you. I live, in-
fidel that I am, and do more to preserve my life than I do to
lose it.

Ah! I die of shame. Is my despair hence only in my
letters? If I loved you as I have told you a thousand times
should I not now be dead? I cheated you. It is you who must
cast blame on me. Alas! Why do you not blame me? I saw
you leave, I cannot hope to see you ever again, and still I
breathe. I have betrayed you. I ask forgiveness. But do not
grant it! Treat me severely! Do not think my feelings violent
enough! Be more difficult to please: bid me I should die of

love for you. I beg you to provide me with this cure, so that I may surmount the weakness of my sex, and end my uncertainties with true despair; a tragic end would no doubt compel you to think of me most often, you would hold fond memories of me, and you would be, perchance, greatly touched by so extraordinary a death. Is death not worth more than the state to which you have reduced me? Adieu, I wish I had never seen you. Ah! I strongly feel the falsehood of this sentiment, and I realize as I write that I would rather be unhappy loving you than never to have seen you; I thus consent without a sigh to my ill-made destiny since you have chosen not to better it. Adieu, promise to miss me tenderly, should I die of pain, and that at least the violence of my passion provide you with an aversion and disgust for all things. This solace will suffice me, but if I must abandon you forever, I would not like to leave you to another. Would you not be very cruel to use my despair so as to render yourself more engaging, and to have it known that you aroused the greatest passion in the world?

Adieu once again, my letters are too long, I lack consideration, I beg your pardon, and I dare hope that you will make allowances for a poor senseless girl, who did not used to be thus, as well you know, before she loved you.

Adieu. It seems I speak too often of my unbearable condition. And yet I thank you from the bottom of my heart for the despair you cause me and I loathe the quietude in which I lived before I knew you. Adieu, my passion grows with each and every moment. Ah! So many things to tell you!

I V

I feel I wrong the feelings in my heart when I try and have you understand them when I write. How happy I would be if you could measure my feelings against the violence of your own!

But I cannot rely on you in this, and I cannot help telling you, far less vividly than I feel, that you should not ill treat me as you do with a shameful neglect that plunges me into despair, and is even shameful to yourself; it is only just that I be allowed to complain of woes I had well predicted when I found you resolved to leave me. I now realize that I deceived myself when I thought you would behave with more propriety than that to which one is accustomed, because it seemed the fervor of my love raised me above all possible suspicion and deserved more fidelity than ordinarily found. But the measures you take to betray me prevail at last on the justice you owe to everything I have done for you. I would be most unhappy to discover you loved me only because I love you and I would want to owe everything only to your heart's inclination; but I am so far from being in this state for I have not received one single letter from you for six months past.

I attribute all this misfortune to the blind abandonment with which I grew attached to you. Should I have not foreseen that my pleasures would end long before my love? Could I hope that you would remain in Portugal all of your life, and that you would renounce your fortune and your country to think only of me? My suffering finds no relief, and the remembrance of my pleasures fills me with despair.

What! All my desires will thus be useless, and never again will I see you in my room with all the ardor and exuberance you had me see? Alas! I mock myself, and I now realize that the emotions that occupied my mind and my heart were in you borne only of a few short pleasures that ended with them. Whilst in these pleasurable moments I should have called my reason to my side to have it moderate the dire excess of my bliss and to announce all I suffer now. But I was yours, and I was in no state to think of what could poison my joy, and forbid me from delighting fully in the ardent expression of your passion. I took too great a pleasure in being with you to think that you would one day be far away from me.

I do remember all the same having told you on some occasion that you would render me unhappy, but these fears would quickly dissipate, and I delighted in surrendering to the enchantment and ill faith of your protestations.

I know well the remedy to all my ills, and I should soon be free of them should I cease to love you. But alas! What remedy is this! No, I much prefer to suffer even greater ills than to forget you. Alas, does this depend on me? I cannot blame myself for having wished even once not to love you. You are more to pity than I am, and it is better to suffer all that I suffer than to revel in languishing pleasures provided by your mistresses in France. I do not envy your indifference, and I feel sorry for you. I defy you to forget me completely, I hold that without me you can but know imperfect pleasures, and I am happier than you for I am better occupied. They have made me, recently, doorkeeper in this convent. All those that speak to me think me mad. I do not know what it is I answer them, and the nuns must be as mad as I to have thought me capable of such work.

Oh how I envy Manoel and Francisco's happiness,[3] why am I not, as they, incessantly with you? I would have followed you, and I would have assuredly served you with more heart. I wish for nothing in this world but to see you. At least remember me. I am content if you remember me, but I dare not be sure even of this, I did not restrict my hopes to you remembering me when I saw you everyday. But you have taught me well that I must be subject to your will. Yet, I do not repent having adored you. I am glad you seduced me. Your cruel absence, and possibly eternal, does not abate the passion of my love! I want for all the world to know it; I do not make a mystery of it, and I am happy to have done all I have done for you against all sense of propriety. My honor and religion is now in loving you fervently all my life, since I have begun to love you.

I do not tell you all these things so you will write. Ah! do not feel obliged. I want from you only what will come from your heart, and I refuse all other signs of love which you could control. I will find pleasure in forgiving you, for you may find pleasure in not taking pains to write, and I feel a deep desire to forgive you all your faults.

This morning, a French officer had the kindness to speak of you for more than three hours. He told me that peace in France has been concluded. If this is so, could you not come and see me and take me to France? But I do not deserve it. Do what will please you; my love herewith does not depend on how you will treat me. Since you have left, I have not had one moment of good health, and I find no other pleasure than in speaking your name a thousand times a day. A few nuns who know the deplorable state in which you have put me, speak of you most often; I leave my room, where you so often came, as little as is possible, and I look forever at your portrait. It is a thousand times more dear to me than life. It gives me some pleasure; but it gives me much pain as well when I think that I may never see you again; why must it be that I may never see you again? Have you abandoned me forever? I am so desperate, your poor Mariana cannot stand much more, she faints in finishing this letter. Adieu, Adieu, please have pity on me.

V

(June 1668)

I write to you for the last time, and I hope to have you
know by the difference of terms and by the manner of this
letter, that you have at last persuaded me that you no longer
love me and so, I must love you no more. Thus I will send
back by first dispatch all I still retain of yours. Do not fear I
may write; I will not even write your name on top of the par-
cel. I have entrusted all these details to Dona Brites, who was
wont to carry secrets far removed from these. I will be less
suspicious of her troubles than of my own. She will take all
necessary precautions to ensure that you receive the portrait
and the bracelets you gave me. Yet, I want you to know that
for some days now, I have felt the urge to burn and tear to
pieces these tokens of your love once so dear to me, but I
have in the past shown such weakness that you would never
have believed me capable of such extremities. Hence, I want
to revel in the pain I had in parting with them, and provide
you at least with some vexation. I confess, to my shame and
to yours, that I found myself more attached to these trifles
than I would care to say, and I felt the need again to call on
my reflections to rid myself of each one in particular, even as
I flattered myself in thinking I no longer loved you, but in
the end we can convince ourselves of anything given
sufficient cause.

I have put them in the hands of Dona Brites; how this cost me in tears. After countless doubts and a thousand reservations unknown to you and with which I will surely not acquaint you, I begged her never to speak of them, never to give them back, even though I might ask to see them once again, and to send them off, at last, without forewarning me.

I came to know the extent of my love only now I have tried my best to cure myself of it, and I fear I would not have dared attempt this had I foreseen such strife and such violence. I am convinced it would have cost me less pain to keep loving you, ingrate though you are, than to leave you forever. I have come to know that you meant less to me than my passion, and I met with strange sorrows while combating it, once your injurious ways rendered you odious to me.

The ordinary pride of my sex did not help my resolve to turn against you. Alas! I suffered your contempt, I would have endured your hatred and all the jealousy born out of your possible attachment for another, I would have had, at least, some passion to combat, but your indifference is unbearable, your impertinent protestations of friendship and the ridiculous civilities of your last letter have shown me that you received all those I wrote to you and that they caused no stirrings in your heart though you have read them all.

Ingrate, I am still fool enough to feel despair at being deprived of the hope I had that they may not have reached you, and were kept from you. I loathe your facile faith. Had I asked you to acquaint me with a sincere truth? Why not leave me my passion? You had only not to write. I did not seek to be enlightened; am I not miserable enough, having failed in making you take some care to deceive me, and no longer being able to excuse you?

Know that I now perceive you are unworthy of my sentiments, and that I know all your cruel qualities. Yet (if all I have done for you merits that you give some small consideration to the favors I ask), I beseech you, write to me no more, and help me forget you entirely. Should you let me know, however faintly, that you felt some dismay in reading this letter, I would perhaps believe you and perhaps also your acknowledgment and your consent would vex and anger me and all this could inflame me. Thus do not interfere with my ways, you would no doubt upset all my plans, whichever way you entered into them.

I do not wish to know the success of this letter. Do not trouble the state for which I am preparing, I am sure you can be satisfied with the ills you cause me, whatever your designs were in rendering me miserable. Do not free me of my uncertainties. I hope to make of them, with time, something more tranquil. I promise not to hate you. I mistrust violent sentiments far too greatly to dare embark upon hate.

I am convinced that I may find in this country a lover more faithful and better made; but, alas! who will grant me love? Will the passion of another satisfy me? Did mine ever hold any power over you?

Will I not learn that a loving heart once affected never forgets the one who quickened emotions unknown and unattainable till then? That all its impulses belongs to its first love. That its first thoughts, its first wounds cannot be cured or blotted. That all these passions that offer help and that take pains to renew and content, promise feelings the heart can no longer experience? That all the pleasures it seeks with no real wish to find them, only serve to show that nothing is more dear to it than the remembrance of its pain?

Why have you taught me the imperfection and unpleasantness of a bond not meant to be eternal and all the hardships that follow violent love when it is unrequited? Why must blind inclination and cruel destiny have us commonly pursue those who desire others? Even if I could hope for some amusement in a new tryst, and found someone of good faith, I pity myself so greatly, that I would feel great scruples to reduce the worst man on earth to a state like the one to which you have brought me. And though I am under no obligation to spare you, I cannot bring myself to exert on you such a cruel vengeance, even if it came from me, by a change I do not foresee.

I seek in this moment to excuse you. I grant a nun does not normally inspire love. Yet it seems to me that were men capable of reason in their choices, they should attach themselves to nuns rather than to other women. Nothing prevents nuns from reflecting incessantly on their passion, they are not distracted by a thousand things that dissipate

and occupy the world. It must be very unpleasant to see the
one we love always seduced by a thousand trifles, and one
must be greatly insensitive to suffer, without distress, that
they speak forever of assemblies, clothing, and promenades.
One is forever exposed to new jealousies, women are forever
obliged to please, indulge and converse; who can be sure
that they dislike such duties and that they service their husbands with extreme distaste and against their will? How they
must distrust a lover who never questions, who easily
believes and who sees them with much trust and tranquility
carry out these duties.

But I do not seek pretences to prove with logic that you
should have loved me; these are mean devices, and I have employed much better without success. I seize upon my fate too
well to try and overcome it; I will be miserable all my life; was
I not thus when I saw you every day? I died of fright that you
might not be faithful. I wanted to see you at every moment
and this was not possible; I was troubled by the perils you ran
when entering this convent. I did not live when you were at
war, I was in despair not to be more beautiful or more worthy
of you; I muttered against the mediocrity of my condition, I
often thought the attachment you appeared to have for me
would harm you in some way; it seemed I did not love you
enough, I was fearful for you of my parent's anger,[4] I was in
truth in the same pitiable state I am at present.

Had you provided me with some mark of passion since
leaving Portugal, I would have made every effort to escape, I

would have disguised myself to go and find you. Alas! What
would have become of me had you shown no concern for
me once I was in France? What confusion! What aberration!
What shame for my family, who I hold dear now I no longer
love you. You can see I allow calmly that I could have been
in a more pitiable state than I am now. I speak to you
reasonably at least once in my life. How my moderation will
please you, and how you will commend me. I do not want
to know, I have begged you write to me no more and I
entreat you once again to do so.

Have you never reflected on how you treated me? Do
you ever think that you owe me more than to any one else
on earth? I loved you like a mad woman: what contempt I
had for all things! Your doings are not those of an honest
man; you must have had for me some natural aversion not
to love me madly, and I let myself be charmed by very
mediocre qualities indeed; what did you do to please me?
What sacrifices were yours for me? Did you not pursue a
thousand other pleasures? Did you renounce gambling and
your hunts? Were you not the first to leave for war? Did
you not return the last? You foolishly exposed yourself to
danger though I begged you to be careful out of your love
for me. You did not seek ways to establish yourself in Portugal where you were esteemed. A letter from your brother
had you leave without hesitation and did I not learn
that during the voyage you were of the best disposition

in the world? One must aver I am obliged to mortally detest you.

Ah! I have wreaked my own misfortunes; firstly I accustomed you with too much sincerity to a great passion, one must affect artifice to be loved; one must seek ingenious ways to inflame and love alone does not yield love. You wanted me to love you, and as you had formed designs you would stop at nothing to obtain me. You would have even loved me had this proven necessary. But you came to know you could succeed in your enterprise without passion, you had no need for it. What perfidy! Did you truly believe you could deceive me forever with impunity?

Should chance bring you back to this country I tell you I would deliver you up to my parent's vengeance. I have lived too long in an abandonment and an idleness that horrifies me and my remorse persecutes me with relentless rigour. I feel too clearly the shame of the crimes you had me commit and no longer bear, alas, the passion that precluded me from knowing its depravity. When will my heart cease to be torn, when shall I be delivered from this cruel confusion?

However, I believe I do not wish you harm and could even consent to you being happy. But how can this be if your heart be well made? I want to write another letter to let you know that I will be more calm once some time has passed. How I will relish condemning your unjust ways once they no longer hurt me, saying I despise you and speaking with much indifference of your betrayal, forgetting all my pleasures and my pains, remembering you only if I so desire.

I grant, you still hold a great advantage over me, that you filled me with a passion that made me lose my mind; but you must not flatter yourself. I was young. I was gullible. They had locked me up in this convent since childhood. I had seen only unpleasant people, I had never known incessant praises before yours. It seemed to me, I owed you the charms and beauty you found in me and had me uncover. I heard good things said of you, everyone spoke in your favor, you did everything to inspire my love.

But finally the spell is broken. You were of great assistance and I confess I had great need for it. In sending back your letters, I will carefully keep the last two you wrote to me and I will reread them again more often than I read the first ones, so that I may not fall prey to my weaknesses. How they cost me dearly and how I would have loved for you to let me love you always. I realize I am still too preoccupied with my chiding and your infidelity, but remember that I have promised myself a more peaceful state and that I will succeed, or I will take against myself some extreme measure which you will learn without much interest. But I want nothing from you; I am mad always to speak of the same things. I must leave you, and no longer think of you, I even think I will write to you no more. Am I obliged to provide you with an exact account of all my varied emotions?

5

THE RETURN

"Sire, I seek nothing for myself, only I beg of you to free my captain that is imprisoned at the Bastille." "And who would this captain be?" replied the King impressed. Louis XIV had expected Chamilly to ask for money and a title, as was the custom. "It is M. Briquemault, Sire. I served under him a long time ago in Portugal. He instructed me in the art of war and formed my youth, so that my services may be agreeable to your Majesty."

NOËL BOUTON, COUNT OF CHAMILLY, FOLLOWING HIS EXPLOITS IN THE
DEFENSE OF GRAVE (1674) AS RELATED BY THE HISTORIAN COURTE EPÉE.

"You knew the depth of my love and of my tenderness and still you could resolve to leave me."

MARIANA ALCOFORADO, LETTER 4

HAMILLY TOUCHED FRENCH SHORES SOMETIME AT THE end of January or the beginning of February 1668.

Chamilly's return took longer than expected. To catch a ship out of the Algarve, he had ridden to Mertola, accompanied by his servants and a small retinue of officers. Boarding a local ship traveling down the Guadiana River toward Villa Real de Santo Antonio, a small port town at the mouth of the Atlantic, he and his entourage had made their way to the Algarve port towns of Faro or Tavira,[1] from where he hoped to board a merchant ship traveling to Marseille.

Storms were habitual at that time of year, and Chamilly's

plans of gaining time must have run afoul when hefty winds and unrelenting rain delayed his departure. Traffic between cities was frequent and soldiers carried news back and forth, which explains how Mariana was able to write Chamilly a second letter while he was still on Portuguese soil. The reluctance of the lieutenant to deliver her letter is understandable when we know the dangers inherent in such a task.

PROBABLY LEAVING HIS SERVANTS BEHIND IN MARSEILLE TO UNLOAD his possessions, Chamilly traveled over fifty miles a day through densely populated villages. After four years spent in the desolate plains of the Alentejo, the undulating French countryside must have felt unfamiliar. Chamilly alighted at his brother's castle on February 9. Battle had been raging since the third, and barely taking time to rest, Chamilly set off for the front, half a day away.

Chamilly reached his brother as Herard was en route to report on his early successes to the king. Louis XIV wanted to witness the progress personally. Surrounded by the famous musketeer d'Artagnan and his companions who served as his bodyguard, the king met the young Chamilly for the first time. Chamilly made a good impression and there would come a day when Louis XIV would say that Chamilly was one of four men to whom he would entrust the country.

With the French troops outnumbered, the prospects of success were slim. But the arrival of Chamilly changed the odds in the king's favor. Chamilly had not been there five days when, acting against express orders from the Great Condé, he seized control of a fortified bastion deemed impregnable. That night, he and his companions sent a flag and thirty prisoners to Condé. The bastion protected the city of Dole and the town aldermen, impressed and alarmed by Chamilly's prowess, capitulated.

Chamilly's younger brother, Eleonord Bouton, who lived in the area, met the brothers at the city gates delivering one of the cities personally to Herard. The remaining cities surrendered almost immediately. Franche-Comté was taken in less than two weeks.

The war now carried itself to Flanders. His exploits at the battle of Franche-Comté had won him the title of marquis and the regiment he had been promised was finally assigned. Mariana's third letter, steeped in despair and sexual longing, probably reached Chamilly sometime at the beginning of February or at the beginning of March as he was preparing to leave. Mail was privatized and there existed a military mail service. A letter from Portugal to France could take months or as little as four days to reach its destination, depending on the winds. Letters were seldom lost and always forwarded if possible.

The hostilities in Flanders were short-lived. England, Holland, and Sweden formed a league against France, forcing

Louis XIV to sign the treaty of Aix-la-Chapelle on May 2. France was now officially at peace. Herard and Chamilly returned to Dijon. Eleonord joined them.[2] Franche-Comté was returned to Spain.

Herard returned to his administrative responsibilities. Eleonord busied himself with religious duties, while Chamilly faced unemployment for the first time in four years. Uneasy with the prospect of having to reenter civilian life, Chamilly cast around for a new opportunity. The French periodical the *Gazette de France*, dated February 23, 1668, provided him with his next venture. Several copies must have been available at Herard's castle, for the paper related the brothers' exploits in Franche-Comté, and having hired a genealogist[3] to record the family's history, Herard would have wanted the information readily available.

One of the articles described an expedition of volunteers being put together by the Duke of La Feuillade. Capable men were invited to participate in a holy war against the Turks, who held the city of Candia, on the Isle of Crete under siege. Candia was the Italian name for Iráklion, the former capital of Crete, and was ruled by Venetians during the seventeenth century. Chamilly's younger brother, Louis, had died on his way to defend the holy site. Perhaps wanting to honor his dead brother's intent, and certainly anxious to return to a battlefield, Chamilly enlisted.

Chamilly would serve under the Great Condé's nephew, the nineteen-year-old Charles Paris d'Orléans, known as

Saint-Pol, who would lead one of La Feuillade's four brigades. Preparations would take place in Paris. Chamilly was about to enter the intricate maze cast by the Condés.

PARIS WOULD NEVER BE CHAMILLY'S FAVORITE PLACE OF RESIDENCE. Four hundred thousand men and women, including forty thousand beggars, a wealthy middle class, merchants, printers, soldiers, legislators, government officials, and aristocracy populated a city that had become the center for military, economic, foreign, and domestic affairs. A year earlier, Louis XIV had designated a chief of police in an effort to control the mayhem, but in 1668 Paris was still a sea of un lit and unpaved streets, subject to floods and looting.

Chamilly's brother, Herard, owned a house at Saint-Germain-des-Prés in the rue Jacob in the parish of Saint-Sulpice, and Chamilly moved in at the end of May 1668. Servants and baggage followed. Most of his belongings were still in Portugal and would arrive with Schomberg, whose convoy was expected sometime in June.

The French officer had been in Paris less than a fortnight when Saint-Pol offered him the command of his brigade. Saint-Pol was the issue of the illegitimate relationship between Anne Geneviève, duchess of Longueville, sister of the Great Condé, and of her former lover, François VI, duke of La Rochefoucauld. La Rochefoucauld had rejected Anne

Geneviève in favor of a younger mistress. Her distress over the affair is believed to be the reason behind Anne Geneviève's spectacular religious conversion at the age of thirty-five. The beautiful, dejected young woman had sought refuge in a new form of Catholicism called Jansenism, which advocated a strict moral and physical restraint.

Saint-Pol, her favorite son, was the product of her dissolute past and of her radical conversion, of her remorse and her passions. Raised in part by his uncle, the Great Condé, Saint-Pol was eager to follow in his uncle's military footsteps. Saint-Pol was more beautiful than handsome. Rowdy, courageous, excitable, and desperate to make his mark, the battle of Candia would be Saint-Pol's first brush with war.

Preparations for the expedition took place at number 5–19 rue de Condé at the Hotel de Condé and Anne Geneviève, desperate to dissuade her son from going to war, enlisted the help of one of her closest friends, Madeleine de Souvré, the marquise de Sablé. The marquise de Sablé would be remembered as one of the guiding intellectual lights of her time. Kind and thoughtful, she was a woman of infinite taste, and she is greatly responsible for defining the role of hostess as we understand it today. She never offended nor took offense. She knew how to dispel arguments before they began, and she cultivated the art of discourse by encouraging discussions that included the sciences, the arts, and philosophy, reserving the inflammatory subjects of politics and religion to her intimate circle of friends. She exercised caution in all things, and the most powerful men of France, including the king, sought her counsel. Her gatherings brought together the greatest intellects of France and often of Europe.

The marquise had been evicted from her home a few years earlier for her role in the Jansenism movement to which Anne Geneviève belonged. The king, who would eventually undergo a moral conversion of his own, was still enjoying a promiscuous lifestyle, and he frowned upon this new interpretation of Catholicism. The marquise, however, was held in such high esteem that even he had shied away from dismantling the movement. The marquise was responsible for Saint-Pol's mother's conversion, and Anne Geneviève had opened her arms and welcomed her friend as her guest at the Hotel de Condé, until the day the marquise could reenter her own home. The marquise now held many of her soirées at the Hotel de Condé, where Chamilly spent his days and evenings strategizing.

The marquise and Anne Geneviève embarked on a campaign to dissuade Saint-Pol from going. But the more they tried to impress on him the weariness experienced at sea, the extent of the peril faced, and the intemperate weather, the more obstinate the young and flamboyant Saint-Pol became. The marquise shared a love of cooking with Saint-Pol's father, La Rochefoucauld, and she often plied father and son with jams and pastries. Her specialty was creating dishes that could be eaten without distorting the face. The marquise was known for her use of sugar in garnering good will, and like the Portuguese nuns before her, it is likely she offered Chamilly a few sweets to win him to their side, or at least insure that Chamilly would protect Anne Geneviève's son, should Saint-Pol remain determined to leave. How aware were Anne Genevieve and Chamilly that the tables had turned? A long time ago, the beautiful Anne Genevieve, had incited her brother, the Great Condé, to revolt, had come to Stenay where Chamilly lived as a young boy, and had tried to destroy Chamilly's father's reputation. Now, years later, she stood before Chamilly the man asking him to forgive and take care of her son. Chamilly would acquit himself well of the task, making Saint-Pol his friend and protegé. Saint-Pol persisted in wanting to go, and forty-six of the hundred young nobles who followed him everywhere also decided to enlist.

The general consensus among scholars is that Mariana's letters began circulating at one of the marquise's evenings. Given Chamilly's recent military exploits and the marquise's vested interest in Chamilly, there is good reason to believe he was invited to join her evenings.

The events were more than mere social gatherings. Over the course of his reign, Louis XIV had cleverly managed to oust aristocrats like La Rochefoucauld from power, relegating them to the sidelines. La Rochefoucauld had abandoned politics and now devoted his time to writing philosophical maxims describing a pessimistic view of mankind. He, and others like him, tested their writings at these evenings, and the soirées served as outlets for the disenfranchised aristocrats who replaced the sword with wit. Filled with strict social practices, hypocrisy, greed, ambition, and the occasional genuine brilliance, the evenings created a new arena in which nobles could excel. These events would eventually be dubbed salons (which means living room in French), but the evenings mostly took place in the hostess's bedroom because living rooms did not yet exist.[4] Houses were filled with huge unheated rooms that did not lend themselves to intimate gatherings. Bedrooms, the smallest rooms in a house, were best suited for playing society games, reading plays, and hearing music performed. Reputations were made and destroyed at such evenings, and one participated at one's risk and peril.

Chamilly, fresh from his time in Portugal and his exploits in Franche-Comté, was perfect potential entertainment. Historians and scholars who believe in the authenticity of the letters suggest that Chamilly, guilty of a momentary lapse in moral rectitude, flaunted the letters in an effort to shine. However, Chamilly's unease in social gatherings, confirmed by the famous memoirist of the time, Louis de Rouvroy, duc de Saint-Simon, his dislike of politics, and his systematic refusal to indulge in self-promotion, suggests that if he did attend the soirées, it is unlikely he shared the letters with the parliamentarians, men of the cloth, scientists, writers, wealthy merchants, poor aspiring artists, and fellow soldiers who frequented the get-togethers. Less skilled at storytelling than Herard, who was known and admired in these circles, Chamilly most likely frustrated the guests by refusing to engage.

Had Chamilly embodied the typical characteristics of seventeenth-century men (greed, ambition, contempt for private matters, and the need to be noticed at any cost), and showed the letters, no one would have thought ill of him. Privacy was not highly regarded. Everything, from the king's latest affair to a man being cuckolded to sensitive military business was conducted under public scrutiny. Louis XIV's ministers were constantly devising codes, secret instructions, and clandestine rendezvous to govern the country.[5] Private and personal letters were continually being copied and passed from hand to hand, circulating from one salon to another.

Chamilly, however, was a decent, courageous, honorable man, whose name would come to symbolize integrity. He would never fall in love again and would wait ten years before marrying and then only out of gratitude and friendship, not out of love. Much of his future life would be spent in prayer. Even though his affair with Mariana would quickly come to be known, he would never publicly admit to it and Saint-Simon, who knew Chamilly, said that he always looked sad. Remorse and Chamilly's friendship with Saint-

Pol, born out of days and nights spent strategizing, is more likely to have compelled Chamilly to speak.

Mariana's fourth letter reached Chamilly sometime during the second part of June 1668, on the eve of his leaving for Marseille to recruit more volunteers. We know this because in her fourth letter, Mariana mentions the Treaty of Aix-la-Chapelle (May 2, 1668). Schomberg left Portugal on the third of June, unaware that the treaty had been signed. The chronology of the letters once again concurs with the facts. By the time Mariana writes in June, six months or more have passed since Chamilly's departure, and she complains that she has not heard from him in over six months.

Chamilly's response, the only one sent since his return to France, probably left with his two Portuguese lackeys. How tempting to imagine Chamilly sitting at a table in one of those narrow Parisian rooms with high ceilings and panelled walls. Candles lit and servants dismissed, Chamilly faced an empty piece of paper unable to write.

Mariana's answer, knowing, final, irrevocable, followed shortly after. Was it this letter that prompted Chamilly to confide in Saint-Pol, if only to warn the youth away from romantic notions? Did Saint-Pol ask to see the others? And were they shown to serve as a reminder of what harm can follow love? Or were they shared out of guilt or the need to confess? Or was it longing?

Saint-Pol may have used the letters to rise in defense of

Chamilly's lack of interest in social graces, or to bolster his friend's reputation. Female conquests often took precedence over military exploits, and Saint-Pol would have thought nothing of showing the letters in an attempt to end any negative comments.

More likely is that Saint-Pol, touched by Mariana's words, felt the need to share them with his mother. Highly sensitive, and extremely close to Anne Geneviève, Saint-Pol would have realized that Mariana's pain echoed his mother's past. From the son to the mother, to the mother's best friend (the marquise de Sablé) and from there, to the intimates of her salon, was a hop, skip, and a jump, in typical seventeenth-century fashion.

This does not explain, however, how Mariana's letters were to become inexorably linked with an habitué of the marquise de Sablé's salon who had nothing to do with Portugal, Chamilly, or Mariana, or how he, Gabriel Joseph de Lavergne, comte de Guilleragues, a courtier and a socialite, came to play such an important role in the letters getting published, or why scholars would eventually credit him with writing the letters.

The answer, I believe, lies in the marquise de Sablé's unnatural fear of germs.[6] The marquise was, among other things, famous for her hypochondria. With the marquise fast approaching seventy, a guest needed to abide by a strange set of rules before being allowed in her presence. An individual, or missives of any kind, could not approach the marquise without having been vetted by one of the four or five doctors always at her side. So great was her dread of germs, she spent weeks, often months, without coming into physical contact with anyone.

The marquise de Sablé also had the queer habit of recording everything. Her primary doctor, the good M. Vallent, collected every piece of writing that was produced by, or brought to, her soirées. He meticulously copied them on fresh pieces of paper so that the marquise would feel safe holding them in her gloved hands. The doctor's portfolios can still be found at the Bibliothèque Nationale de France in Paris. Called on to copy Mariana's letters for fear they might carry some unknown disease, the good doctor would not have known how to translate the colloquial expressions used by Mariana, understood by Chamilly but unintelligible to someone unfamiliar with Portuguese. The good doctor would have wanted the letters to be perfectly understandable before passing them on to the marquise. He happened to know the perfect man to help him.

Joseph Gabriel de Lavergne, called Guilleragues by his friends, was considered an "honest" man, which is to say he epitomized the virtues of manners and propriety extolled in polite French society. Worldly, loved by everyone, obsessed with his lineage to the point of being vain, extremely witty, an opportunist continually in debt who made it his business to be informed of all the latest gossip, Guilleragues was a favorite across the salons of Paris.

Like Chamilly, Guilleragues' association with the marquise of Sablé also came from the Condé family. Having led a rakish life in Bordeaux as a young law student, carousing and amassing debts, Guilleragues was heading toward an uninspired life when an old classmate hauled him out of his debauchery and landed him a job with the prince of Conti, the youngest brother of Anne Geneviève. Like many of his fellow aristocrats, the prince of Conti had abandoned his military aspirations, and, in his case, had secured a reputation as a generous patron of the arts. Guilleragues quickly gained favor with the prince, organizing his soirées, handling delicate diplomatic matters, and representing him on official business. When the prince married, so did Guilleragues. Through the prince's artistic inclinations, Guilleragues, who had impeccable taste, became an avid connoisseur of playwrights, poets, and writers. But the prince died in 1666, leaving Guilleragues without a job and a source of income. Abandoning his wife and newborn in Bordeaux, Guilleragues made his way to Paris. Capitalizing on his connections with the Condé family, he obtained access to the marquise, in the hope that he might secure a job through her contacts.

Two years into his stay in Paris, still unemployed and facing financial ruin, Guilleragues tried writing in the hope of being published, reviving an old English game called "Valentines." The game consisted of writing the names of thirty men and thirty women on separate pieces of paper and putting them into separate bags according to gender. A third bag was filled with sixty little sayings that related a sentimental situation. Guilleragues wrote the romantic sayings in the form of little poems known as epigrams or madrigals. Names and a poem were drawn and read aloud. The fun came from the strange juxtapositions this created. Guilleragues' lighthearted satirical songs and limericks were not enough, however, to warrant a publication. With time on his hands, eager to please, and decidedly hungry for some novelty, Guilleragues was, of all of the marquise's habitués, the best positioned to help the good doctor find a translator.

A few weeks earlier, on May 18, Guilleragues had caught the opening of a play, *The Mad Quarrel*, presented by Molière's company. The play had been written by an old friend of his, an ex-actor called Subligny, who was ideally suited for the task Guilleragues had in mind. Guilleragues knew Subligny from the days when Subligny worked as an actor for the then-unknown Molière, who, busy touring the provinces, had been invited to perform his plays for the prince of Conti. Guilleragues, responsible for orchestrating the performances, had befriended Subligny.

Subligny, wisely abandoning the acting profession to become a writer, had followed Molière to Paris. Hired by a famous publisher called Claude Barbin to report on European events, Subligny wrote a weekly pamphlet using rhymed couplets to cover the stories of the rich and famous. One of his most recent issues recounted the marriage of Marie-Françoise to Dom Pedro.

The credit for the translation of the letters has often shifted between Guilleragues and Subligny and though it is possible that Subligny had a rudimentary knowledge of Portuguese, neither was capable of translating letters written entirely in Portuguese. Scholars therefore presumed the letters must have been written by one of them, most likely Guilleragues, never stopping to consider Mariana's knowledge of French and the possibility that she would have written the letters in Chamilly's vernacular, interspersing them with Portuguese expressions familiar to Chamilly. Guilleragues probably corrected grammatical errors while Subligny translated the odd Portuguese or Spanish term. This would explain why the names of Subligny and Guilleragues are both mentioned in connection with the letters.

WHILE GUILLERAGUES RETURNED THE LETTERS TO THE GOOD DOCtor for him to pass on to the marquise, Saint-Pol took leave of his mother, departing from Paris at the end of August to join his friend.

The young prince reached Chamilly in Lyon where the soldiers had been ordered to gather on August 24. A week later they left for Toulon. Ships were cheaper to rent than horses, so the troops sailed the river Rhône until Avignon, reaching their departure point at the beginning of September.

Chamilly and his men finally boarded the *Serene*, one of three ships paid for by the king, on September 20. There exists a wonderfully improbable story, published three years after the expedition, found in one of the journals describing the voyage to Candia, in which a priest grabs the letters from Chamilly and throws them in the ocean. Chamilly, on seeing them sink, pays a young sailor a great deal of money to dive into the waters and save the letters.[7]

As sails rose to the sounds of the sailors' chants, in Paris, Mariana's words cut directly into the marquise's heart. Mariana's letters recalled a pain the old marquise had spent her life trying to erase. She too, like Anne Geneviève, had been abandoned. For years, the guests at the marquise's soirées had sought to define the very nature of love, but her way of life served to hide a deeper pain.

Before reaching the age of twenty, the marquise, forced into an arranged marriage, had married a man forty years her senior. Her aged husband had seduced her only to abandon her shortly thereafter in favor of a younger woman. The marquise had tried to retaliate by taking on a lover, but he too had abandoned her. Struggling through countless pregnancies, stillbirths, and infant mortalities, depressed and humiliated, she had taken refuge in the provinces. Time and her husband's death had eventually returned her to polite society, and she had made it her life's work to establish her superiority based on how she lived, spoke, behaved, entertained, and socialized. She had kept love at a safe distance ever since, preferring to discuss the evanescent nature of amorous feelings rather than to participate in them. Mariana's words spoke to her and to every other betrayed woman in Paris.

From copy to copy, from salon to salon, the letters gained in popularity. According to clues found in a novella published a few years later, a princess had dared a courtier to write passionate letters. The princess, quickly identified as the Princess Henrietta of England, sister-in-law to king Louis XIV, famous for supporting the arts, was Guilleragues' mentor. The princess loved pranks and games of all kinds and scholars believe that she prompted Guilleragues to write his Valentines. With Mariana's letters circulating, it would have been very much in character for her to dare Guilleragues to write his own version of the passionate Portuguese letters.

Scholars who contend that the letters are written by Guilleragues largely base their thinking on the discovery of a novella titled *The Story of La Violette or of the False Count of Brion*, by Jean de Vanel, published sixteen years after Mariana's letters. The main protagonist, La Violette, is a swashbuckler accompanying the Duke of Savoie in an extraordinary mission to Lisbon. There, he meets a nun claiming to be the author of the letters: "One day being at a

Comedy, [. . .] he (La Violette) found himself seated next to a veiled lady; and waiting for the play to begin, began conversing with her: 'Portuguese Ladies,' he told her, 'are very fortunate to be able to travel without being known.' 'This privilege,' answered the stranger, 'does not go very far; we are only allowed to hide our faces; but French Cavaliers hide their feelings so well that we are nearly always mistaken.' [. . .] 'If one must believe the Portuguese Letters, we know how to love much better than men . . .' '[T]hose letters,' said the false merchant, 'are but a game and the work of a man at the court of France that wrote them under orders from a Princess to show her how a passionate woman could write.' 'How can you speak thus ingrate,' replied the stranger raising her voice, 'you who have in your possession the originals of the letters and who can not forget that I wrote them to you while you were in Paris, when you returned there after the peace of the Pyrenees?' "

If we are to believe the writer of the novella, the letters are from a lady from Lisbon and the action takes place shortly after 1659 after the signing of the Treaty of the Pyrenees. These details bear no resemblance to the time or situation described in Mariana's letters. The details do, however, mirror the contents of a second set of Portuguese letters that were published as a sequel, in Barbin's second print run of Mariana's letters. This second set of letters is a pastiche of Mariana's letters, without the depth or psychological insight of the originals. Ignored by scholars because of their lack of literary merit, they are closer in style and in content to the seventeenth-century fashionable love letter. These are the letters most likely to have been written by Guilleragues in answer to Princess Henrietta's dare to match Mariana's passion.[8]

Deeply in debt, needing to make money, with his own set of love letters, Guilleragues suddenly had enough material to get published. Publishers paid anywhere from fifty to three hundred pounds (roughly between 25 and 134 U.S. dollars) for a good piece of writing, enough to tide him over for half a year. A published work would raise his credibility among aristocrats and perhaps, at long last, lead him to a job.[9]

Armed with his letters and his Valentines, Guilleragues must have approached Subligny once again, this time to ask for an introduction to Subligny's publisher, Claude Barbin.

The Parisian bookseller Barbin, and a favorite publisher of French aristocracy, was renowned for his ability to launch books. His shop was strategically located on the second porch leading up the very busy steps to the Sainte-Chapelle and the Palais de Justice in Paris. In the corner next to the main entrance of the church, Barbin stocked a good variety of books in a series of small interconnecting six-by-eight-foot rooms. He published Molière, La Fontaine, La Rochefoucauld, Boileau, and others who were the thinkers, poets, and playwrights of his time. Always in wait of his next possible hit, he kept abreast of the latest creations. He stood at the periphery of literary gatherings, gleaning information from friends, clients, and the authors who circulated their works at soirées like those held by the marquise de Sablé.

It is not known if Guilleragues approached Barbin or if Barbin contacted Guilleragues. All that can be surmised is that sometime in October 1668, the two men came together over a little wood stove and the copper container used to burn the coals that warmed Barbin's shop. Sitting in two comfortable fabric chairs positioned to encourage clients to browse, amidst fake plaster busts painted rust to imitate bronze and easels announcing Barbin's latest titles, Guilleragues and Barbin discussed the possibility of publishing Guilleragues' writings. A clever man, Barbin must have insisted that Mariana's letters be part of the deal.

Did Guilleragues hesitate to include Mariana's letters? Certainly the men were still negotiating when, on October 28, 1668, Barbin climbed the steps leading to the royal archives seeking a royal privilege (the equivalent of securing an option in today's terms)[10] for a book entitled *Portuguese Letters.*

THAT NIGHT, CHAMILLY WAS STILL AT SEA. A VIOLENT STORM FORCED his ship, the *Serene,* to drop its sails and hove to. The mast on the *Diamond*, the ship ahead in Chamilly's fleet, had snapped. Forced to steer west in order to follow the damaged ship and supply it with goods, the *Serene* sighted the Cap d'Escade, the longest point on the island of Crete, the following day. Screams of joy resounded across the deck. A few more days and they would reach their destination.

The situation in Candia was more tenuous than expected. The garrison of the town was without any leadership. The captain responsible for overseeing of the city's defense had taken ill. La Feuillade and Saint-Pol found themselves having to take command of the whole garrison. A few hundred French soldiers faced three thousand Turks. On November 13, two weeks into their stay, Chamilly ordered his men to make their way to the barricades two at a time in order to create continuous fire in the direction of the enemy. The position was so precarious the men crawled on their bellies to and from the site.

Three weeks later in Paris, Barbin was busy registering a series of works:

> This day the seventeenth November 1668 has been presented to us a King's Privilege given in Paris the 28th of October for a book titled Valentines, Portuguese Letters, Epigrams, and Madrigals by Guilleragues.

Barbin and Guilleragues had struck a deal. Barbin needed Guilleragues as much as Guilleragues needed Barbin. Getting published added to the chances of Guilleragues getting a job. Barbin could not publish Mariana's letters without using Guilleragues' name. The law required that an author be cited when registering a privilege. Mariana's last name was unknown and if Barbin was to publish her letters, he needed an author. Guilleragues' name proved useful in two ways: it answered the question of authorship and, as important, helped circumvent the tricky subject of censorship.

Three factions claimed supremacy over censorship: the Church, the king, and the legislative parliament. All three fought each other for the right to control unpublished materials. Religious practices permeated every aspect of social life. The impious nature of Mariana's love letters, if real, crossed a dangerous line. If the letters were fictitious, the content became less threatening. Throwing doubt on the authenticity of the letters protected Chamilly's identity and Barbin from future recriminations.

The amount of text to be published was substantial and would take several weeks, if not months, to typeset and get ready for printing. This was time Barbin could not afford. There was no way of knowing when the Candia expedition would end, and Barbin needed the letters published while Chamilly was away. With Christmas fast approaching, printers would be in even greater demand than usual. Barbin would publish Guilleragues' love letters and the Valentines at a subsequent date.

As the originals have been lost, we do not know if Mariana's letters were dated. Barbin positioned the first and last letters, easily deciphered in their proper position, and then placed the remaining three in order of size from the shortest to the longest. Barbin's order jumbles the facts so thoroughly, it is one of the primary reasons scholars have been so slow in recognizing the letters as genuine.[11]

By mid-December, Chamilly and his superiors knew they could not sustain their efforts much longer. They determined to gather all the remaining soldiers and undertake one last full attack. Saint-Pol, who spoke Italian fluently, was put in charge of recruiting men from the other factions. He was only able to secure another fifty. On December 16, two hundred and eighty combatants attended mass at three in the morning. They took position for battle one hour later. Hidden in a huge metal bonnet at the foot of the entrenchments, they waited for the signal. The cannon fired eighteen times followed by a firebomb. The French soldiers attacked so vigorously, the enemy buckled under the attack. But the odds were too great. Within a few hours the fields were reddened with the blood oozing from mutilated bodies. Chamilly saw his cousin, René de Saulx-

Tavannes, fall next to him. Saint-Pol was difficult to contain. Inebriated by the sight and smell of blood, the youth kept removing his armor and plunging into the fray. Chamilly spent as much time ordering him to keep his armor on as he did protecting Saint-Pol from the Turks. The French fought valiantly and foolhardily the whole day. The battle ended at nine o'clock that night. Chamilly was severely wounded in the leg. He had been struck in the face two weeks earlier. He was lucky; many had been killed and few survived their wounds. Chamilly would not fight in subsequent attacks. Saint-Pol walked away unscathed.

BARBIN RECEIVED THE FIRST DRAFT OF THE BOOK THE WEEK BEFORE Christmas. Paris shut down for the holidays, and Barbin would not be able to deposit the copies before the beginning of January. He spent Christmas with his future wife, looking forward to the year ahead.

CHRISTMAS DAY, IN ONE OF THE CHAPELS OF SAINT-TITUS, CANDIA'S cathedral, Chamilly was awarded the order of the Guardian Angel. Created the year before by Pope Clement IX, the title was given to those who waged war against the Turks. The soldiers had paid a heavy price for the honors bestowed on them. The men's efforts had yielded few results, and it was decided that the time had come to return home.

Chamilly's brigade started to board on January 6, but it took another eighteen days before favorable winds allowed them to leave. By then, Saint-Pol had contracted a severe fever. The voyage would be long and painful, with fever spreading throughout the ship. Alighting in Malta, Saint-Pol made his way to Italy by horse and then rode to Paris. Chamilly stayed with the men and finally reached Toulon March 18.

Two months earlier, on January 4, copies of a little book called *Lettres Portugaises traduites en français* (*Portuguese Letters Translated into French*) were duly deposited at the parliament. That same week, the book could be found on the shelves of Claude Barbin, Bookseller, in Paris. The book sold out in a matter of days. The success was resounding. A counterfeit edition was printed in Cologne before the month was out. Guilleragues and Chamilly were mentioned by name in the counterfeit editions. Controversy raged. Were the letters real or imagined?

Claude Barbin had a hit on his hands.[12]

6

CHAMILLY

"And wilt thou have me fashion into speech
The love I bear thee, finding words enough,
And hold the torch out, while winds are rough,
Between our faces, to cast light on each?"
ELIZABETH BARRETT BROWNING
SONNETS FROM THE PORTUGUESE (1850)

"It may be you will find greater beauty, but never will you find such love,
and all the rest is nothing."
MARIANA ALCOFORADO, LETTER 1

HAMILLY LANDED IN TOULON IN MARCH, HAVING
taken care of his sick men until the last day of
the voyage. Avoiding Paris, Chamilly joined
Herard, who was in Luxemburg. On July 8,
1669, Chamilly received the command of his first regiment.
The Regiment of Burgundy counted twenty-four companies
totaling two thousand men, and it held the forty-seventh
rank in the infantry.

In Paris, Chamilly's name was becoming synonymous
with passion, and his military exploits were adding to his
fame as a lover as well as glamour to the letters. Barbin was
preparing his second print run. This time he would include
Guilleragues' letters and publish Guilleragues' *Valentines*
under a separate cover.

Chamilly stayed well away. The next year found him in Dunkirk readying his regiment. For the next two years Chamilly disappeared from the public eye, but by 1671, the knowledge of the letters was so widespread, any passionate letter was referred to as "a Portuguese."

Returning to his domains, Chamilly began a long over-due inventory of his possessions, but he could not resist the prospect of battle.[1] Joining his brother at the seiges of Burick (June 3, 1672), Wesel (June 4), Groll (June 9), and Deventer (June 21), against the Dutch, he fought brilliantly under Herard's command. As always, the brothers caught the eye of the king.

The king liked attending battles and so did the aristo-crats of Paris. Hordes of interested spectators made their way to faraway fields to witness men being killed. Gilded carriages lined up one after another, filled with men and women applauding the sight of blood as if attending a play. Among them watched the young and ambitious François-Michel Le Tellier, marquis de Louvois, the king's recently appointed minister of war. Louvois perceived the Chamilly brothers as a threat to his power and was relieved when Herard passed away unexpectedly in 1673; he was only forty-three and about to be named a Marshal of France. Louvois' fears and jealousy now turned toward the thirty-seven-year-old Chamilly.

By 1674, Chamilly was back in Paris and though it was

Barbin's last year as sole owner of the rights, that year he did not publish the letters.

Chamilly dealt with the loss of his brother the only way he knew how. He threw himself in the way of danger. He asked to be named governor of the city of Graves, the most precarious stronghold of France, and the king complied. The stronghold regrouped all the cannons and ammunition of other abandoned posts. Louvois secretly proposed to Chamilly that he sell the ammunition surplus to make a profit. Sensing he was being set up, Chamilly pretended to comply but never did what Louvois asked.

The stronghold of Graves came under attack by the Prince of Orange, ruler of Holland the year Chamilly took over. The siege lasted four months and became the most followed event of the French court and population. News from the front reached the capital daily. The country remained riveted as Chamilly defended the city against the Dutch army.

His men were fervently devoted to him. He would often apologize for putting them through hardships. Louis Étienne Dussieux, in his *History of Great Generals*, relates how, every time Chamilly was appraised of the enemy's progress, he would answer, "Who cares?" or, "All the better, this means they are closer to our swords." The men used the saying constantly and wrote songs about their beloved commander. Chamilly won the extreme loyalty of his men by always keeping them informed of his plans. From the lowliest soldier up to his commanding officers, everyone knew what movements were planned for the night or the days to follow. The soldiers felt secure in the knowledge of what was coming. Chamilly would often send violin players into the trenches at night, to keep his men entertained. When a soldier did well, Chamilly promoted him regardless of the soldier's station in life. He insisted that his men not take their hats off in his presence, stating he would be honored to count any one of them among his friends. He handed out his own money to his men and he shook their hands in a sign of friendship, a gesture unheard of before him.

Officers and soldiers alike were willing to die for him, and even when the men were eventually reduced to eating their horses, they made jokes about it and declared it a delicacy. They stood behind Chamilly, who refused to capitulate.

An officer in his garrison abandoned his post with the idea of deserting. Caught, fellow officers ran to Chamilly to demand a punishment. Realizing the morale of his troops would be jeopardized if an officer were shown to be a coward, Chamilly coldly replied, "You fight well, judge better. He followed my orders and I had my reasons." The following night, he called on the officer in question, who threw himself at Chamilly's feet begging forgiveness. Chamilly sat with him through the night talking about life, honor, duty, and second chances. From that morning onward, the young officer became the bravest of his men and volunteered for the most dangerous of missions. Impressed, his fellow officers apologized for having thought him even capable of desertion. The young man became so fearless that Chamilly was forced to order him publicly to take greater care of his life.

Four hundred Dutchmen arrived to take over a neighboring island. They had already intercepted five boats filled with wine intended for Chamilly's men. Chamilly's cavalry and three hundred footmen traveled by night and made their way to the riverbank facing the island. The water was deeper than he had anticipated and, realizing his men would have to swim across, Chamilly threw himself in the water, sword in hand, shouting to his men, "We pass or we die." He was five or six yards away from the shore when a Dutch officer took aim in his direction. Seizing a fellow officer's pistol, Chamilly wounded the Dutchman and grabbed the enemy's gun. Helping seven of his men to climb the branches of a tree, he was about to join them when he heard screams. His men were drowning. Diving back into the water and swimming across, Chamilly ordered all the horses in. Seizing the drowning men, he pushed them onto the horses, forcing them to grab the saddles. All of his men made it. By daybreak, Chamilly had recaptured the boats and the men were laden with wine and food.

The Prince of Orange's honor was now at stake. He called

in the whole of his army. Cut off from rations, Chamilly was running out of food. One house was left standing. Citizens of the town and soldiers lived underground in caves. Paris hung on Chamilly's every action. The king ordered him to capitulate but he refused and that week Chamilly left another two thousand Dutchmen lying wounded or dead on the battlefield. France was mesmerized. The enemy had lost sixteen thousand men to his hundreds. Once again, the king ordered him to capitulate. Chamilly could no longer feed his men and had no choice but to comply. He departed with the greatest honors bestowed upon him; Chamilly was the most famous man in France.

On his return, the king granted him a wish. It was customary to ask for and receive a moneyed title in such circumstances. "Sire, I seek nothing for myself, only I beg of you to free my captain who is imprisoned at the Bastille."

"And who would this captain be?" replied the king, impressed and surprised. (Louis XIV had expected Chamilly to ask for money and a title, as was the custom.)

"It is M. Briquemault, sire. I served under him a long time ago in Portugal. He instructed me in the art of war and formed my youth, so that my services may be agreeable to your Majesty."

The request was a direct affront to Louvois, who had refused to compensate Briquemault for his services to the country. When an offended Briquemault had thrown his commission into Louvois' carriage, Louvois had thrown

Briquemault in jail. Imprisoned at the Bastille, the most dreaded prison in France, Briquemault was suffering from harsh treatment and would have died were it not for Chamilly's intervention. He was freed within a week of Chamilly's request. Chamilly's selfless act only added to his prestige, and Louvois was humiliated. He saw to it personally that despite Chamilly's extraordinary exploits, he was not selected as Marshal of France. Chamilly would have to wait another thirty years before receiving the honor.

Chamilly remained busy with war for the next two years. On April 22, 1676, he was severely wounded. Unable to fight, he accepted an offer to govern the city of Oudenarde. His wound stopped him from joining the campaign of 1677 and it was during this time that he met Isabelle du Bouchet, the daughter of the wealthy merchant Jacques Bouchet and Magdeleine d'Elbène. Twenty years his junior, extremely pious and reputed to be incredibly ugly, she nursed Chamilly back to health. At the height of his fame, when Chamilly could have chosen any woman he liked, he offered his hand to the grateful Isabelle, saving her from the life of a spinster. Theirs was a marriage of convenience, though time brought the couple together, at least as friends. Saint-Simon described her as

extremely virtuous and pious without ever imposing her religion on others. She was extremely witty with a refined sense of humor made for the world, poised and self-possessed, at ease, spirited without ever overstepping the bounds of decency, modest, polite, discerning and with all this sensible, much good humor, nobility and even magnificence, she was always devoted to good works though one would have thought her forever busied with the world. Her conversation and her ways made you forget her singular ugliness. She and her husband were always extremely close.

Isabelle du Bouchet remained devoted to Chamilly all her life, following him from post to post. She rescued him financially more than once and endeared herself to Louvois, who could not resist her wise and discreet ways. Chamilly was, at last, made Marshal of France on December 4, 1704, and was anointed a Knight of King's Commanders (Chevalier des Ordres du Roi) on February 2, 1705. The king said of Chamilly that he was one of four men in whose hands he would entrust the country. His reputation was such that, in 1697, a book intended for the young who "sought a career in the military" was dedicated to him. The title, *The Perfect Man of War or the Description of the Accomplished Hero,* was meant to describe Chamilly. His picture graced the first page of the book, and the dedication and preface were to and about him.

Chamilly had spent his life at war. Wounded numerous times including blows to the head, he eventually drifted into senility. Saint-Simon, who met Chamilly when Chamilly

was already in his seventies, described him as a man filled
with honor and heart but also sad and so aged, he was
nearly "imbecile":

> They were both rich and without children. His wife,
> who knew all things, languished to see him suffer. He
> had served young in Portugal and the famous Por-
> tuguese Letters were addressed to him. They were
> written by a nun he had known who had gone mad
> for him.

Chamilly was alone with a priest when he died on Tues-
day, January 8, 1715, at the age of seventy-nine. No one
knows what passed between him and his priest as he received the last sacraments. His body was transported from
his home on Rue des Petits Augustins (a street that no
longer exists) in the Faubourg Saint-Germain, to his parish
church of Saint-Sulpice. Two distant cousins attended
the burial. He is interred in the chapel of Notre-Dame du
Treilly.

He never denied his affair with Mariana. The memorial-
ists at the time all considered him the receipient of the letters. He never tried to stop the counterfeit editions that
mentioned his name. The two women who had been part
of his life died a few months apart from one another. While
Isabelle du Bouchet was ill and bedridden, the Letters once
again came into print in Paris. She died on November 18,

1723, at the age of fifty-nine, after outliving Chamilly by eight years. During Chamilly's lifetime, forty-nine editions of the letters were published. A print run for Barbin usually represented around fifteen hundred copies. At the time of Chamilly's death as many as fifty thousand copies were probably in circulation. No one knew Mariana's full name or if she even existed.[2]

7

THE LETTERS, A CONTROVERSY

"And do you know what happens? We do not wish to cede what we debate. By dint of looking for reasons, we find them, we speak them out loud; and after, we cherish them, not so much because they are good, but to avoid contradicting ourselves."

FROM THE BOOK *DANGEROUS LIAISONS* (INSPIRED BY THE PORTUGUESE LETTERS), LETTER 33, BY CHODERLOS DE LACLOS. 1781

"Love, consider well your lack of foresight. You were betrayed and you betrayed me."

MARIANA ALCOFORADO, LETTER 1

ARIANA'S LETTERS HAD TAKEN ON A LIFE OF THEIR OWN. Ten editions were printed the first year: four from Barbin, the rest were counterfeit editions produced in Amsterdam[1] and Cologne.[2] The book measured 5½ inches long (14½ centimeters) by 3 inches wide (8 centimeters) and fit in the palm of a lady's hand. The cover was a deep burnt-red made out of a luxurious cowhide. The book contained 188 pages. Each page held approximately twelve lines and each line contained on average three words. The book slipped easily into a vest and a lady could hide it underneath her fan.

Barbin, aware that he was treading on dangerous territory, shrouded the lovers in mystery, creating a frisson that played to current tastes. His preface recalls the "Roman à clef"

(coded novels) that were thinly veiled accounts of court life, in which the characters sported anagrammed versions of their real names. Aristocrats already familiar with the letters would have known that Barbin was referring to Chamilly, and that the use of the word "translator" was a euphemism for Guilleragues' role in the letters coming to print.[3]

To the Reader

I have found means with much care and effort to recover a correct copy of the translation of five Portuguese letters that were written to a young man of good family who served in Portugal. I have seen all those who know themselves in the affairs of the heart either praise them or seek them out with such haste that I thought I would give them a singular pleasure in having them printed. I do not know the name of the one to whom they were written, or of the translator, but I felt they would not be displeased were I to render them public. It is most unlikely that I have been able to present them without some errors that may disfigure them.

Preface of 1669 to the book, *Portuguese Letters*[4]

Fashion alone, however, cannot account for the extraordinary success of Mariana's letters. Mariana's words addressed a deeper societal need. They spoke to a romantic injustice. Until her letters, a tacit silence surrounded men's behavior. Mariana's letters broke the code, upsetting the balance of power between men and women. According to the French scholar Jean-Michel Pelous, "the dazzling success of the *Portuguese Letters* allowed French society to become aware of what its own image of love was lacking. In this sense they are at once a crystallization of a latent dissatisfaction and a sudden revelation of new sentimental horizons."[5]

Women set the tone in polite society, yet their reality clashed with the refined world they created. In order to sublimate the injustices inflicted by men, the marquise de Sablé coped by elevating manners to a cult. Her feelings of dejection may have been one of the primary causes for her hypochondria. Her fear of death was so great, she employed a doctor to sit next to her at night to shake her at regular intervals just in case she slept too deeply and did not wake up. Her only protection against heartache and disillusion was to invent a world in which men had no choice but to behave according to her rules.

Anne Geneviève, the duchess of Longueville, Saint-Pol's mother, addressed her feelings of rejection with equal extremes. Using religion to protect herself, she retired from the world at the age of thirty-five, foregoing both sex and love. She sublimated her sexual longings by wearing a chastity belt and by sleeping on stone floors.[6] Radical behaviors, like those of the marquise and Anne Geneviève, were necessitated by the lack of any legal or moral protection against abusive behavior.

Mariana's letters legitimized these women's life experiences.[7] For the first time, the female reader was allowed to acknowledge both betrayal and erotic feelings. It is not surprising, therefore, that men felt it necessary to dismiss and trivialize Mariana's letters, as did a review written by a lawyer who served as secretary to a famous literary society, only seven months after the publication of the letters:

> Would you like, said Oronte, to judge a book by its title? It seams [sic] to me, he continued, that there are excellent ones that are rotting in the shops, while others who are worth nothing sell out. Look no further than the Portuguese Letters. Isn't it surprising how many copies have sold? And I see no other reason than, if not the charm of novelty, that it was pleasant to read the letters of a nun, however they were written, without considering the title is the game of a deceitful publisher, who is only looking to shock the public.— "What care you," interrupted Cléante "if they are real or not, as long as they are good? Are they not very tender? Believe me, take what is given, whichever way it comes, as long as it is worth reading, and let us not be like those braggarts who do not wear gloves unless they come from Martial. —"There is no doubt, answered I, there is some tenderness in these letters, if you consider the Oohs and Aahs, but if by that you mean feelings

you will be hard pressed to find two remarkable ones. And in truth, is it not a great misery that we should read a book that says so little? Anyway, there is no style; the sentences run on forever, and what bores me most is the endless repetition, harping over what only merits to be said once. Frankly this is what disgusted me. For I am not, as you believe, of those who find nothing good unless it is guaranteed authentic.[8]

Considering the profession of critic did not yet exist, the fact a review was published at all speaks to the impact Mariana's letters had on French society.

A famous grammarian of the time, Pierre Richelet, rewrote the letters entirely before including them in his anthology of *"The most beautiful letters of the French language."*[9] The French scholar Jacques Chupeau states the letters are, "modified, reshaped, watered down: they are distorted. As shocking as these corrections may appear today it has at least the merit of underlining the originality of the stylistics of the Letters and the creative freedom of the writer."[10] Every reference to a convent, a nun, or sex is gone. The success of the *Portuguese Letters* could not be dismissed; therefore, it was re-appropriated.

Years later, in 1748 philosopher Jean-Jacques Rousseau was still trying to diminish the power of the letters:

Women in general do not like art, are versed in none and have no genius for them. They can have success with small works that demand only lightness of spirit, taste and grace. But that celestial fire that warms and brazens the soul, that genius that consumes and devours, that burning eloquence, those sublime emotions that carry their marvels to the bottom of our hearts, leaves always to be desired in women's writings. They cannot describe or feel love. . . . I would bet everything in the world that the Portuguese letters were written by a man.[11]

When, one hundred and fifty years later, the Franciscan monk Jean-Francois Boissonade finally revealed Mariana's name to the world, the case appeared closed. Historical findings proved Mariana had existed. She was officially credited with having written the letters, and they were filed under her name at the Library of Congress in Washington, D.C. Then, in 1926, a stunning piece of information was discovered. The American scholar Frederick C. Green unearthed the registration for the royal privilege Claude Barbin had obtained in order to be able to publish the letters.

"This day the seventeenth November 1668 has been presented to us a King's Privilege given in Paris the 28th of October for a book titled The Valentines, Portuguese letters, Epigrams and Madrigals by Guilleraques."

"Now, I suggest," said Green, "that Barbin was a clever publisher who, realizing the market value of a publication . . . of clandestine amours of a supposed nun, published as genuine, letters, which were written by Guilleragues. In the preface, as was so often done in the seventeenth century by the lesser novelists, he attempted to lend a greater interest to the fiction by mysteriously inferring that it was drawn from real life."[12]

Green's discovery brought Guilleragues' name back to the forefront: "In the absence of more complete knowledge as to his writings, however, there is nothing but conjecture to justify the assumption that he was the Guilleraques who wrote the Lettres Portugaises."[13]

Jacques Rougeot and Frédéric Deloffre met Professor Green's challenge in 1962. Compiling Guilleragues' voluminous correspondence, they pieced together a comprehensive biography of his life, and carried out an extensive analysis of the text proving, in their opinion, that Guilleragues was the author. Their 1962 book, *Portuguese Letters, Valentines and other works by Guilleragues,* still dominates scholarly thinking today.[14]

From then onward, Guilleragues was recognized as the author of the letters. Countless papers, memoirs, and conferences placed the letters firmly in the cultural and literary context of France. All efforts to establish a scenario in which the letters could have been written by Mariana were abandoned. In its stead, is the widely held belief that the affair took place, that it became known in Paris, that "they knew of the betrayal of the officer and the passionate letters sent by the nun. Did Guilleragues read these letters?

We do not know. It suffices that he dreamt what they must be."[15] As Henri Coulet remarked, it seems as though "an esthetic study of the work was able to begin only once the authenticity of the letters were brought into question, that is to say once the letters were considered a cohesive endeavor and concerted effort by an author."[16]

Rougeot and Deloffre's case for considering Guilleragues the author relies on the following discoveries and assertions:

1. The registration of the privilege discovered by Professor Green.

2. Guilleragues was unemployed but found a job as letter-writer to the king ten months after Mariana's letters were first published.

3. A small book, *L'amour échappé*, published in November 1669, by Donneau de Visé seemed to confirm their thinking. It describes Guilleragues under the pseudonym Philarque: "Philarque is good looking, quick witted and most pleasant in company. He is very erudite, he composes rhymes very well, as well as love letters."[17]

4. Rougeot and Deloffre cite two sources as possible inspiration; an inventory of Guilleragues' father's books included the Latin poem "Héroïdes," which they believe Guilleragues could have read as a boy. The second source is an unpublished work by the marquis de Sourdis, a regular of the marquise de Sablé's salon, entitled "Thirty-two Questions on

Love" in which five of the thirty-two questions have to do with the concept of abandonment.

5. Rougeot and Deloffre's internal analysis of the letters note that the letters have strange and unorthodox rhythms; this, they explained, is due to Guilleragues' innovative use of language even though Rougeot and Deloffre acknowledge that Guilleragues' abundant correspondence shows him to be a writer, extremely conscious of form.

French scholar Jacques Chupeau's subsequent discovery of the novella, *The Story of La Violette or of the False Count of Brion,* suddenly supplied Rougeot and Deloffre with a reason prompting Guilleragues to write.[18]

If there is no doubt that 'this man at the court of France' that Vanel gives as author of the Portuguese Letters is Guilleragues, it is just as easy to identify the 'Princess' who, according to him, would have inspired the work. He refers, of course, to Henrietta d'Angleterre . . . She encouraged Boileau. Racine was her favorite poet. There is nothing surprising in the fact that she distinguished the merit of their friend Guilleragues that she protected since 1666 . . .[19]

Emmanuel Bury, professor at the University of Versailles–Saint-Quentin, believes that Guilleragues not only wrote the letters for the princess but also his game of Valentines.

He sees the novella as a proof the letters were written on a whim, and he suggests that to pass from "gallant banter (the Valentines), to the expression of love (the Letters)," is not such a leap, and that, "Guilleragues and his friends go from one artifice to another."[20]

Rougeot and Deloffre conclude:

> Guilleragues may not be what we commonly refer to as a genius, but the "lettres portugaises" are surely a work of genius borne out of a refined society, dedicated to the study of the human heart, joining an acute sense of the realities of love to a sense no less admirable of modesty and of human dignity, capable of consigning the result of its clear sighted analyses under a precise and artistic form. We (Deloffre and Rougeot) like to think that a society judged only reasonable and only witty has produced a work that represents it most by giving literary form to a banal, desperate love.[21]

ROUGEOT AND DELOFFRE AND SUBSEQUENT SCHOLARS' ASSERTIONS merit reexamination, starting with the registration of royal privilege dated November 17, 1668.

Alain Viala's book, *Birth of the Writer,* explains that Barbin's decision to use Guilleragues' name was pragmatic and born out of necessity. Viala brings to light the laws that governed publishing, meant to protect the author: "Since 1571, the law stipulated that the name of the author be indicated." There was only one way in which a publisher did not have to name the author. Viala explains that in 1669, if a publisher put together an anthology that consisted of a "series of works by *different* authors, the publisher could publish this anthology under the heading of a *single* writer."[22] Viala goes on to say: "Sometimes even an author took the initiative of putting together an anthology. The privilege was then established in his name."[23] The list mentioned by Barbin in the registration of the privilege can therefore be interpreted as an anthology containing both Guilleragues' and Mariana's writing. By creating an anthology and using Guillerague's name, Barbin met legal requirements without having to produce Mariana's full name, which Barbin did not know. Viala's research opens the door to a new interpretation of the privilege. When Barbin lists "The Valentines, Portuguese letters, Epigrams and Madrigals by Guilleragues," he is listing a "series of works by two different authors coming under the heading of one single author."

Guilleragues is not the author of Mariana's letters. He is responsible for creating an anthology of works that include Mariana's letters.

Barbin renewed the privilege for the letters in 1681; He does not include the Valentine's or mention Guilleragues'

name. Even without Viala's discovery Rougeot and Deloffre's conclusion that Guilleragues is the author creates major incongruities.

If the letters are a work of fiction, how is it that they mirror Mariana's story with such exact historical accuracy?
Without any knowledge of the Portuguese language, geography, or way of life, how could Guilleragues have known
to use the consecrated expression "the balcony from which
we can see Mertola," referring to an old roman archway a
few yards from the window of Mertola and not to the city
thirty-three miles away? If Guilleragues was such an ex-
traordinarily gifted writer, why are the letters his only work
of fiction? These are only a few of the inconsistencies that
arise if we accept that Guilleragues was the author of Mariana's letters.

The pieces of the puzzle only begin to make sense if one
takes into account the unclaimed *second set of letters.* If one
accepts Guilleragues was (as Rougeot and Deloffre discovered him to be through their research) a lowly aristocrat
always in debt, looking for any opportunity to advance
himself, Mariana's letters become the catalyst that
prompted Guilleragues to write a *second set of letters* in response to a dare. It is important to note that the *second set
of letters* and the book *Valentines* came out the same day,
August 20, 1669. Barbin used Guilleragues' second set of
letters in a second "augmented" edition of the Portuguese
Letters, and because there were not enough valentines to

make a book, Barbin added a text he had previously published. (The book includes *Questions of Love* by Roger Bussy-Rabutin, who happened to be Chamilly's old commander, as well as a few personal letters by Guilleragues).

Barbin also used Guilleragues' *second set of letters* to skirt the issue of censorship.

A seventeenth-century manuscript discovered in 1982 suggests that the amalgamation of Guilleragues' letters and Mariana's was indeed a subterfuge. The manuscript combines both sets of letters. Guilleragues' letters are positioned first, followed by Mariana's letters, and the letters are numbered one to twelve as if to indicate they are part of the same story.[24]

Guilleragues became letter-writer for the king only once the *second set of letters* was published though this particular position had been vacant for some time.

The book, *L'amour échappé* by Donneau de Visé, was published on November 12, 1669, and can therefore refer to Barbin's August publication of Guilleragues' *Valentines,* and to the *second set of letters*.

On closer examination of the manuscript, *Thirty-two Questions on Love,* the date seems blurred. Instead of November 1667, as Rougeot and Deloffre state, it can also be read as November 1664.[25] The marquise de Sablé was without a home in November of 1667, living in the Hotel de Condé, as well as being in the middle of the huge religious polemic concerning Jansenism that also involved Anne Geneviève.

November of 1664 seems a more appropriate time for the questions to have been written, as they come on the heels of La Rochefoucauld and the marquise de Sablé's maxims, when she and her friends spent their days discussing all things to do with love. Guilleragues was still in Bordeaux and in the employ of the prince of Conti, busy with administrative affairs. Other than this text, further research has yielded next to nothing as a likely source of inspiration.[26]

One can interpret Vanel's novella as referring to two sets of letters:

"Those letters," said the false merchant, "are but a game and the work of a man at the court of France that wrote them under the orders of a Princess to show her how a passionate woman could write!" "How can you speak thus ingrate," replied the stranger raising her voice, "you who have in your possession the original letters . . ."

Both protagonists are correct. Vanel refers at once to the second set of letters written by Guilleragues on a dare and to Mariana's original letters to Chamilly. The story continues and the lady refers to herself as coming from Lisbon, suggesting Vanel was mostly inspiring himself from Guilleragues' second set of letters, whose nun is in fact a canoness. (A lady belonging to any one of several religious orders who lived under a rule but not under a vow and could come and go as she pleased.)

Scholars argue that as a Portuguese nun, Mariana was not capable of writing the letters in French.[27]

A new scholarly field in pluri-lingualism, developed over the last decade, strongly suggests that Mariana would have been more than capable, and that in fact her writing in French is the most likely scenario. Groundbreaking discoveries dealing with how languages interact with one another help us understand how Mariana wrote in French while at the same time infusing the letters with her native Portuguese rhythms.[28] The originality and strength of the writing, so troublesome when attributed to Guilleragues, becomes self-explanatory if one accepts that Mariana wrote in French. According to Chantal Zabus, the odd rhythms like those found in Mariana's letters are in fact traces of a foreign language.[29] Zabus suggests that by bending a dominant language (Mariana's Portuguese) to certain artistic demands (writing in French to be understood by Chamilly), one introduces new cultural material into the second language. In Mariana's case, she bent, or shaped, the French language to meet her emotional needs.

If a person resides in an area where several languages live side-by-side, the different languages influence one another. Mariana lived in a war-torn country, in a garrison town, where soldiers from France, England, and many other nations coexisted. This influx of foreigners presupposes that Mariana was exposed not only to different cultures but also to different languages from the day she was born.

Zabus goes on to demonstrate (and this is crucial in the case of the Portuguese letters) that a language can be superimposed onto another, or if you will, that traces of another language can be found in a text, for example in the choice of an expression or in the way a sentence is structured. This explains why, when the Portuguese were finally allowed to translate Mariana's letters into Portuguese (they had been banned for 150 years), Portuguese scholars thought the letters were originally written in Portuguese. The Portuguese language naturally embraced Mariana's rhythms because they were Portuguese rhythms to begin with. Mariana enriched the French language with rhythms emanating from her own maternal language.

Anecdotal evidence speaks in favor of Mariana knowing French. French was taught at the convent. Schomberg learned Portuguese in three months.[30] Because of the absence of overstimulation, languages were easily acquired. Documents of the time tell stories of soldiers walking into cities and learning new languages in a matter of weeks.[31] Noblewomen were expected to master a second language.[32] Mariana, like every other nun in Europe, would have been versed in Latin, and French was the preferred language of European courts, including Portugal. French soldiers were stationed in Beja as early as 1664, and Mariana would have been expected to be able to converse with them in French in order to secure possible donations. Her father was friendly with the Portuguese ambassador to France. The convent owned French books and a French saying was carved into one of the stone archways of the convent. Portuguese society was freer, less sophisticated, and more apt to openly express emotions. Placed into the hands of someone like Mariana, the French language freed itself from its superfluities and was allowed to take on a new kind of flight that would inspire generations to come. The letters, considered surprising within the French context, belonged in a world where the fado, a melancholic and passionate love song, was the lament of kings and peasants alike.³³

Emmanuel Bury argues that the pertinence of the letters today is the best proof that the letters are a work of fiction. I believe the opposite. Authenticity does not negate literary merit. Mariana's self-awareness is no less significant because it is real, and her clarity elevates and crystallizes the language into an artistic form.

For my part, Guilleragues' cleverness does not reside in his having written the letters but in recognizing their worth. Historical prejudice and ignorance concerning the context in which Mariana was able to produce the letters sent scholars in the wrong direction.

Guilleragues went on to become the French Ambassador to Turkey. He remained continually in debt. His diplomatic skills helped smooth over difficult relations between the two countries. He was the first to establish what is now known as diplomatic immunity. Always looking for ways to save money, he insisted that ambassadors be exempt from paying import-export taxes (a tradition still in place today). He died penniless, leaving his wife and daughter with no other resource than the protection of his friends. "Neither Racine nor Boileau, nor any other academician ever sang his praises."[34] While he was ambassador, he hired a young man, Antoine Galland, for thirty cents a day, to peruse Persian writings, perhaps in the hope of discovering another literary treasure. Guilleragues' wish came true. Antoine Galland came across *The Arabian Nights*, and spent the next twenty years translating them. Galland regretted not being able to put *The Arabian Nights* under the protection of his mentor, "the most capable of appreciating and of helping recognize the true worth of beautiful things."[35]

A valentine today signifies a gift or card, sometimes satirical, often anonymous. We may not remember Guilleragues' game or his rhymes, but they are largely responsible for popularizing a tradition we enjoy to this day.

We owe much to Guilleragues. His keen observations on art found in his abundant correspondence, his deep friendships and support of artists, and his admiration for their craft, explains how he came to recognize the value of the letters. He may well have translated a few expressions or at least regularized some spelling, but for the most part, he knew to leave the letters alone. The letters have enriched the French language. They are and should be considered a French masterpiece, not written by an unemployed forty-year-old man in answer to a dare, but by a twenty-eight-year-old Portuguese nun, desperately in love. Mariana's time spent as scribe, faithfully recounting the nuns' religious forty-hour periods, followed by years of keeping exact accounts of goods and prices, amply prepared her for writing these letters. We must be grateful to Guilleragues and Mariana. Her letters inadvertently prompted some valentines to be published, and Guilleragues' infinite good taste allowed a great work of art to reach us through time and controversy, unscathed and untouched.

8

MARIANA

"The length of our passion no more depends on us than the length of life itself."
DUKE OF LA ROCHEFOUCAULD (SAINT-POL'S FATHER), CIRCA 1664

"Will I not learn that a loving heart once affected never forgets the one who quickened emotions unknown and unattainable till then?"
MARIANA ALCOFORADO, LETTER 5

LLEGAL COPIES OF THE LETTERS BEGAN CIRCULATING IN Portugal months after they were published in France, yet there is no mention of Mariana's letters in the convent archives or in official documents. The year the letters were published, in 1669, a prior in charge of discipline visited Mariana's convent. He came from Xabregas to investigate suspicious behavior and verify that the convent operated under strict religious rules. He stayed only a few days, returned home, and wrote copious notes regarding the various abuses and infractions. He sent letters exhorting the nuns to behave and ordered severe punishments. Mariana's affair is not mentioned, but serious infractions never were. No one would have betrayed or

testified against Mariana because to do so would have exposed the convent to financial ruin. Rich nobles would have stopped sending their daughters through the gates.

Convent records do show that Mariana became doorkeeper in 1668. A man, who served as butler, operated the main door at the convent. Mariana was most likely responsible for a door inside the convent as it seems unlikely that the nuns would have wanted her at the servants' and goods' entrances, running the risk of her having contact with the outside world, though that too is possible. If the nuns took pity on her, they may have sought to distract her. Only conjecture surrounds the reasons why she was given this position and it can either be viewed as a punishment or as an effort to help alleviate her pain.

The year Mariana's letters were published, 1669, Dom Pedro signed an edict sending nuns back behind bars. Laws passed that year instituted the death penalty for those guilty of entertaining questionable relationships with nuns. Students caught visiting convent parlors were banned from attending universities. The freedom the nuns had enjoyed during the war was revoked. Peace brought back bishops from Rome.

Little from Mariana has reached us. Her signature can be found on convent records and on a few invoices. These are preciously kept at the Regional Museum in Beja, situated on the convent premises, where the window of Mertola is intact.

The accounts registry from February 1674 bears this

note: "Gave a tostaô to the mason who installed Madre M. Alcoforado's bars." The windows of Mariana's little house were barred, a decision probably coming from the provincial priest in charge of the convent.

Mariana ran for the office of abbess twice in her lifetime: once in 1706 and then again three years later in 1709. The first time she garnered one vote, the second time she lost by only ten. She took on the position of vice-abbess. Her little sister Perigrina, who wrote in her will that she owed everything to Mariana, eventually went on to become abbess.

Legend has it that Francisco Alcoforado had the windows of his house facing the convent shut down when illegal copies of Mariana's letter began circulating. They were to remain that way for the next hundred years. The Alcoforado name disappeared within a few generations. The estate and Alcoforado properties were sold.

The last nun died in 1892. Edgar Prestage, a British historian of note, visited the convent in April of 1894 and found the convent in process of demolition. He says that, "Curiously enough, the tradition of Mariana and her fatal love has been perputuated in the convent and city, in spite of the attempts, legitimate enough, on the part of monastic chronicles and others to hide all traces of it." The remains of the great convent of Concieção were transformed into Beja's Regional Museum in 1927. The street where Mariana spent the first years of her life still exists. The year

Mariana died, in 1723, sixty-three editions of her letters had been published, one edition for every year since Chamilly had left her, plus two.

Proof of Mariana's existence first came to us through her death certificate. It perhaps best exemplifies how even in death, there was a need to mystify. The official registry lies about Mariana's age, probably so no one would know she had entered religious life too young. Yet one thing in the death certificate remains true from Mariana's letters. From the day Chamilly left, Mariana's health deteriorated. The convent document states:

The 28th day of the month of July 1723 has died in this Royal Convent of Conciecão Mother Dona Mariana Alcaforada at the age of eighty-seven, all years passed in the service of God. She was always very regular at choir, and at sororeties and she fulfilled all her duties. She was exemplary, no one found fault with her for she was kind to everyone. She did rigorous penance for thirty years, suffered great infirmities with patience always looking to suffer more, and when she realized her last hour had come, she asked for the sacraments, which she received in a state of perfect consciousness giving thanks to God for having received them. She ended her life, giving signs of predestination and speaking up to the last hour, in proof of which, I, Dona Ania Sophia Batista de Almeida, Secretary of the Convent, wrote this, which I signed on the same day, month and year as above.

From the convent archives,

This Wednesday (28 July) was buried Mother D. Mariana Alcaforada.
Grave & slaked lime six hundred reis 600
For nine masses; one at one hundred and
   twenty, eight at one hundred and fifty 1,320
For the Royal eggs (pastry) given to the priests,
   sugar and eggs bought 140
For the wine given to the priests and friars
   during their stay at the convent 450

Those who buried her did not know she would outlive them all and that however much they would try to make her disappear, her words would survive slander, speculation, anonymity, and controversy. They continue to voice a pain that resonates with all those who wait in vain for a loved one to return. Her letters acknowledge that we may seek to reach the stars, but that in matters of the heart, nothing ever changes.

And then . . .

Dom Afonso VI, King of Portugal (1643–1683)

Following the advice of two Dominicans and a Jesuit, Dom Afonso confessed to his impotence, and allowed his marriage with Marie-Françoise to be annulled. After being detained for some time in Lisbon, Dom Afonso was exiled to the island of Terceira (an island off the Azores), where he remained for some years enjoying relative freedom with permission to hunt and spend time outside. Dom Pedro, forever worried his brother might attempt a coup, eventually brought him back to Portugal and locked him up in the Castle of Cintra, formerly a royal palace, that was transformed into a prison. Dom Afonso died December 12, 1683 at Cintra.

Alcoforado, Balthazar Vaz (1645–1716)

A document dated August 29, 1669, discovered by the Portuguese scholar Manuel Ribeiro, and quoted in his *Vida e Morta de Madre Mariana Alcoforado*, speaks to the pressure Balthazar underwent shortly after the letters began circulating illegally in Portugal. Written and administered on behalf of Mariana's father by the notary Manuel Martin de Fonseca of Beja, the document states, "I give to my son, Balthazar, who has decided to enter the clergy of his own free will at the age of twenty-four, a dowry. . . ." Eight months after Mariana's letters were first published in France, and a few months after they had reached Portugal, Balthazar forfeited his military career, lost his inheritance, and entered religion.

Balthazar left Beja to enter a monastery in the town of Beringel where he eventually became prior in 1716. According to the stipulations of Francisco's will, Balthazar, who was now a priest, had to forfeit all his rights to the Alcoforado estate. Balthazar fought his father on this and refused the possibility of dividing the estate between him and his brothers. The situation escalated to the point where Balthazar brought the case to court. Francisco died in 1676 without anything having been resolved. Balthazar was executor of the will and refused to comply with its terms. He contracted a fever, believed to be malaria, in 1710 that would plague him the rest of his life and from which he would eventually die.

Priesthood did not deter Balthazar from fathering three illegitimate children, two sons and one daughter named Leonor Apolónia. He placed his daughter in Mariana's care, and registered her as the daughter of his youngest brother, Francisco, who was Chief Judge of the district court.

Balthazar collected rifles and owned wonderful hunting dogs. His most prized possession was a rifle given to him by the Duke of Medina Sidónia. The Duke had used this particular rifle in his first battle for the county of Niebla where

Balthazar had enlisted. The people of the county were incensed that the Duke had given this rifle to Balthazar, and historians believe this may be because the general population, aware of Balthazar's involvement with Mariana's affair, frowned on his behavior. Balthazar willed the rifle to a nephew with instructions never to sell or give it away.

Balthazar finally won control of the estate in September of 1716, having spent forty years battling Miguel. Four months after having legally taken over as administrator, Balthazar died on Christmas morning. He never tolerated slander of any kind, and he remained known for his jocular humor. An amusing text of his is still available at the Evora Library in Portugal. His calligraphy is stunningly beautiful. He wrote his own will, and his weakened hand still expresses fortitude of character. The most telling line is perhaps the one found at the end of his testament. He writes: "Never was a greater sinner born."

Alcoforado, Francisco da Costa (?–1676)

Francisco continued to favor his son Miguel. There is no way of knowing if he ever saw Mariana once the affair was discovered. Certainly official knowledge of the affair was suppressed and never commented on. Francisco may have had a hand in destroying all documents pertaining to Chamilly's presence in Beja and throughout Portugal. While an important number of documents can still be found chronicling exploits of French officers at that time, only one document mentioning Chamilly survives. Though this is highly speculative, some historians believe the affair was squashed. At Francisco's death, a document listing debt owed to him was found. Some of the most influential men in the country were on the list, and it is possible that Francisco bargained for protection from the scandal, offering to cancel debt in exchange.

Alcoforado, Miguel (1649–1727)

Miguel pursued a brilliant military career, and married young. He placed his daughters in a convent at the opposite end of town from the convent of Conciecão where Mariana and Peregina lived. He remained friendly with Dom Pedro.

Alcoforado, Perigrina (1660–1741)

Perigrina took care of Mariana until the day Mariana passed away. When Mariana's dowry ran out, Francisco refused to help, and Perigrina stepped in, helping her older sister financially, saving Mariana from ruin. She was elected abbess from 1730 until 1732. She was kind and respected by the nuns. For many years she was responsible for writing obituaries. She painted vivid and accurate portraits of the nuns, enriching the normal arid style employed at the time. She died from a malignant fever that lasted three days.

Barbin, Claude (1628–1698)

Claude Barbin died in Paris, having sold books all his life. At his death, in his shop were seventy-two copies of the Portuguese letters in two volumes and approximately one hundred "packets" of the Portuguese letters for sale. He died a relatively poor man, despite his brilliance at marketing and his having published some of the greatest literary figures of his time. *The Portuguese Letters* was Barbin's bestseller.

Bouton, Nicolas (?–1662)

Chamilly's father, Nicolas Bouton, came from impoverished gentry and spent his life intent on boosting his family's fortune. A pageboy for seven years at the court of Queen Marie de Medici, Nicolas traveled to Holland, where he served under Maurice de Nassau. He had just finished training as a musketeer, when his parents called him home insisting that he get married. He spent his life at the service of the prince of Condé. He had fourteen children and of his nine sons, Chamilly was the only one to reach old age.

Briquemault, Henri Baron of, Seigneur de Saint-Loup, (?–August 16, 1692)

Eleven years after Chamilly had Briquemault freed from the Bastille, Chamilly's old commander and friend was forced to leave France. Louis XIV had decided to forbid all Protestants from practicing their religion by revoking the decree of Nantes of 1685. Until now, the decree left individuals free to practice their religion of choice. No longer welcomed as a Protestant, Briquemault sought refuge in Berlin, and was instrumental in taking care of the political refugees who, like him, were flooding in from France. He is buried in the Cathedral of Wesel, Germany. His coat of arms is placed on his tomb.

Castelmelhor, Luis de Vasconcelos e Sousa (1636–1720)

Dom Pedro, fearful Castelmelhor might instigate Dom Afonso to revolt, banished Castelmelhor from Portugal. Traveling to France and Italy before settling down in London in 1677, there he served queen Catherine of Braganza (sister to Dom Pedro). He was allowed to return to a province of Portugal in 1685, and then to Lisbon in 1687. Dom Pedro readmitted him to court, and he became one of his most trusted advisers.

Condé, Louis II de Bourbon, fourth Prince of Condé, the Great Condé (1621–1686)

The Great Condé eventually retired from the military, finishing his life in his castle at Chantilly surrounded by great poets like Racine and Boileau.

Conti, Armand de Bourbon, prince of (1629–1666)

Brother to the Great Condé and of Anne Geneviéve, the Prince of Conti was protector of Guilleragues. A great patron of the arts, he fostered Molière's career.

D'Ablancourt, Frémont-Jean-Jacob (dates unknown)

Louvois, in an attempt to tarnish Turenne's reputation with the king, sent a special envoy to Portugal to destroy Frémont d'Ablancourt's credibility. Schomberg, having been informed of the plot, warned d'Ablancourt, who was able to outsmart his enemy.

Dom Pedro II (1648–1706)

Dom Pedro took over the government on November 23, 1667. Fearing a possible backlash from the population, instead of taking on the mantle of king, he chose the title of Prince Regent. He and Marie-Françoise married on April 2, 1668. He always dressed in black as per the tradition of the country. He only ever drank water, refusing any alcohol, and demanded abstinence from everyone around him. He was very temperate in his diet; he ate small portions and sometimes ate sitting on the floor with a piece of cork under him, with only one person in attendance. Fidalgos who had drunk wine were not allowed at court that day. Despite his apparent severity regarding others' behaviors, Dom Pedro indulged in promiscuous sex, and had commerce with prostitutes and African slaves. It is believed he suffered from a sexually transmitted disease. Like his brother Dom Afonso, Dom Pedro was passionate about bullfights. Shortly after Marie-Françoise's death, he married an English girl, Maria Sophia Elizabeth, daughter of Philip William, Duke of Nieubourg. She was said to be very beautiful and did not wear rouge like the Portuguese noblewomen, who were known for smothering their faces with red paint (make-up). Dom Pedro slowly redressed the country's dissolute ways, and took on the title of King of Portugal at the death of Dom Afonso.

Gunzman, Luisa (1613–1666), Queen Regent

Mother of Dom Afonso, Dom Pedro, and Catherine of Braganza, she had eight children in all.

La Rochefoucauld, Francois de, (1613–1680)

After participating in the Fronde, La Rochefoucauld rallied around the King and was re-invited to court. Spending the rest of his life frequenting salons like that of his good friend the marquise de Sablé, he is remembered for his incisive maxims on the human condition. (Our virtues are often but our vices in disguise.) A painful disease brought him close to blindness and he was cruelly affected by the loss of his son, Saint-Pol, whom he cherished above all else. His maxims were published by Claude Barbin.

Longueville, Anne Geneviève de Bourbon, Condé (1619–1679), and Longueville, Charles Paris d'Orléans, Count of Saint-Pol, then Duke of Saint-Pol in 1671 (1649–1672)

Anne Geneviève's religious fervor grew more intense over time, and she divided her days between the religious institutions of Port-Royal des Champs and the Carmelites in the faubourg St-Jacques. Her beloved son Saint-Pol died at the passage of the Rhine into Germany with the French army on June 12, 1672. Anne Geneviève's brother, the great Condé, brought back his body wrapped in his coat, and deposited the youth at her feet. Anne Geneviève never truly recovered from her son's death.

Louis XIV (1638–1715)

King of France and Navarre from 1643 to 1715, his reign was filled with excess and splendor, impressive military and governmental achievements. He favored and promoted the merchant class, whose unconditional loyalty he could buy, over aristocracy, ironically providing the lower classes with the intellectual tools enabling a new understanding of inequities and fostering resentment in nobility that would lead up to the French revolution. He is remembered as the Sun King.

Louvois, Francois Michel Le Tellier, Marquis of (1639–1691)

Louvois won the King's confidence through flattery. After the death of Turenne, he took over the military. Founder of French military schools, he is famous for reorganizing the army. Brutal and authoritarian, he tried to exercise influence in areas other than the military without much success. Were it not for the diligent efforts of Chamilly's wife, Louvois would have refused to name Chamilly Marshal of France.

Dona Brites Francisca de Noronha (1662–1712)

This is the nun believed to have been Mariana's confidante and friend during the episode of the letters. Approximately the same age as Mariana, she was wealthy and she eventually became abbess of the convent. Governing with intelligence and heart, Dona Brites was responsible for a huge expansion in the convent, including the building of a church and an oratory in the name of the Holy Eucharist. She left the convent toward the end of her life for the town of Caldas in the hope of obtaining medical help for a generalized pain, but with no success. She returned to the convent of Concieção a few years before her death at the age of seventy-two.

Sablé, Madeleine de Souvré (1599–1678)

The marquise de Sablé died peacefully at the ripe old age of seventy-nine. She requested to be buried in her parish cemetery as a commoner without pomp or ceremony. Her name remains tied to the greatest luminaries of her time. Her gatherings instigated vital contributions to politics, religion, and literature. The letters are part of her legacy.

Savoie, Marie-Françoise-Isabelle de, Princess d'Aumale, Mademoiselle de Nemours (1646–1683)

Marie-Françoise conceived a daughter within the first year of her marriage to Dom Pedro but never gave birth again, though she lived for another fifteen years. Her only child died at the age of twenty-one, a few months before she was due to leave for France to get married. After moving to Portugal Marie-Françoise never returned to France.

Schomberg, Frederick Herman, duke of (1615–1690)

Named Marshal of France, Schomberg was forced to leave France for Portugal in 1685, at the revocation of the decree of Nantes. His first wife having died, he married a Portuguese noblewoman, but then left for England, where he was named duke of Tetford. The king sent him to Ireland to stop King Jack II. On July 11, 1690, having fought eight squadrons and reduced King Jack's army to flames, he was killed by a riding saber piercing his body followed by a pistol shot through the head.

Turenne, Henri de La Tour d'Auvergne, viscount of (1611–1675)

Turenne is remembered as one of France's greatest generals. Originally a Protestant, Turenne is the one responsible for enlisting Schomberg and then Briquemault in the Portuguese war. He personally approved every officer that was sent over, including Chamilly. He eventually converted to Catholicism. He was profoundly good and tolerant in a century ruled by impiety and fanaticism. He lived amongst his soldiers without affectation and never gave in to court politics. He always maintained that diligence and expeditiousness were the two main qualities for success in a battle. A great believer in personal responsibility, he shared victories with his troops but blamed only himself for any losses. He would always say "I lost" to a poor outcome or "We won" to a great one. He died at the age of sixty-four, killed by a stray cannonball that ripped an officer's arm off and hit him in the chest.

Mariana's Letters

The letters officially crossed the English Channel nine years after they were first published in France. Entitled *Five love-letters from a Nun to a Cavalier. Done out of French into English* this translation by Ro L'Estrange was published in 1678. They were extremely popular and subsequent editions of the letters followed. Richardson credits the letters as the inspiration behind his novel *Clarissa*.

Banned from Portugal by Dom Pedro, who ordered that the letters be described as fictitious if they were mentioned, the letters would wait one hundred and fifty years to be translated into Portuguese. They were published for the first time in Portugal in 1819.

Translated into Spanish, Russian, German, Italian, and numerous other languages, they remain as poignant today as they were when Mariana wrote them.

Genealogy of the Alcoforado Family

Francisco Alcoforado—Leonor Medes
Ana—1638, two boys, two girls
Mariana—1640–1723
Balthazar—1645–1716, two illegitimate sons and one il-
legitimate daughter
Catarina—dates unknown
Miguel—1649–1727
Francisco—1655–?
Filipa—1658–?
Maria (Perigrina) 1660–1741

Genealogy of the Chamilly Family

Nicolas Bouton—Marie de Cirey
Had nine boys and five girls. The first two died in the crib, the third was premature and did not survive. The fourth, Jean-Bernard, was the first to survive infancy.

Jean-Bernard—25 September 1625–1645, died from fever contracted after his first battle.

Phillipe—13 November, 1626—died young

Charlotte—27 November, 1627, became a nun in 1644, and abbess in 1684

Herard—13 January, 1630–1673

Gabrielle—24 March, 1631–1661, died shortly after getting married.

Antoinette—22 April, 1632, became a nun

Marguerite—15 March, 1635, died in infancy

Noël Bouton—6 April, 1636—1708, no children

Nicolas-Eléonord—10 February, 1638, died 1706

Louis—10 November, 1640, joined the order of Malta in 1659.

Anne-Françoise—7 April, 1647

Thirty-two
Questions on Love

by the Marquis de Sourdis

(These questions were passed around in the salons for the guests to read and then debate.)

1. Is it better to lose a person we love to death or to infidelity?
2. Is it better to have free access to a person we love, but that does not fully return our love, or to be perfectly loved by someone who is not free to see us?
3. Is greater jealousy a sign of greater love?
4. Is desiring a "thing" more delicious than owning it?
5. Is the union of two hearts the most appreciable and greatest pleasure in life?
6. Are love and desire two opposite feelings?
7. Can we love someone who loves another?
8. Can we stop loving a person who does not fully return our love?

9. If a woman breaks off with a man she loves on a whim, for the sake of more freedom without loving anyone else, if she wants to get back together, should the man accept?

10. Should two people who love each other tell each other their suspicions of jealousy without the use of coldness and ill humor?

11. If a lover is jealous without reason, should the partner make it real, even if others talk?

12. Is the love of a girl (virgin) more violent than that of a woman?

13. What is the lesser crime in love, to be refused or not dare to ask?

14. Can love survive on its own for very long?

15. Can we love for love's sake without expectations?

16. Can we love something more than ourselves?

17. Is the trouble free pleasure of not loving as pleasing as love itself?

18. Which kind of love is more delicious, that of a girl, of a married woman, or of a widow?

19. What kind of love is more agreeable: that of a virtuous woman, or of one that is less than virtuous?

20. Can an honest man, without compromising his sense of ethics, avenge himself on a woman who was unfaithful?

21. What is the greater crime? To publicly boast of ac-

tual favors given by a woman, or boast of invented favors from a woman who gave none?

22. Can a man, who is secretly loved by a woman, insult a rival who does not know he has one?

23. Can a man be as passionate about a woman whom he knows has loved before, than a woman who has never loved at all?

24. Does a woman insult the man she loves by seeking help from another man?

25. Should a woman hate a man she loves who does not consent to help her, knowing he is otherwise engaged?

26. Is it reasonable for a woman to ask for details of a previous affair before she gives marks of affection to a man, and should the man comply?

27. If a man received gifts from a woman, should he return them if she decides to leave him and asks for them?

28. Should a man ask for personal gifts that can be recognized by others from someone he loves and if he leaves, should he keep them, return them, or burn them?

29. Should a woman give a man she loves personal gifts, when he asks for some?

30. Which is better, to win a woman through her heart or her intelligence?

31. If a man knows a woman he loves wants to leave

him, should he let her go freely after having told her politely that he knows her designs, or should he keep her by threatening to cause a scandal?

32. Should a man ever cause insult or displeasure to a woman he loved, for any reason whatsoever?

The Game of Valentines

Guilleragues' game of Valentines was a favorite of the salons. Here is Barbin's preface with a few examples.

The game of Valentines was invented a long time ago; but it is only recently that we make them rhyme: here are those that have fallen in my hands. One must, to play correctly the game of Valentines, put the name of thirty men and of thirty women, on sixty separate pieces of paper, and also copy the madrigals separately. After having pulled the name of a woman and a man, we pull two madrigals to see what they say. If they are things very far from one another, or very accurate, the different effects of chance can sometimes be pleasant, and I hope that this selection of epigrams on all kinds of subjects will amuse you.

III
You are filled with good intentions,
And you claim it your profession
Not to listen to sweet flattery.
You say flirts are not the thing,
Yet that is what you are, darling.

VIII

You can count on my discretion
Too many reasons make me shy,
Even if you want to admit our indiscretions,
I will make sure to deny.

XIX

You are unfaithful, I can tell,
And so a strange vow I will voice,
To no longer live this hell,
But Alas, if I do change,
Will I find a better choice.

XXIX

I must retire without complaint,
It is true, I should not be jealous.
I chide you without reason, precious,
I was your fifth lover, you want only four,
It is normal that you do not want to open every door.

XXXI

An eternal love scares you,
You do not mind if we love you,
But you fear a lengthy fury,
And my passion so extreme,
Causes me greater ennui,
Than the rival I so envy.

XXXII

I am keeping your jewels, and I say we are quits,
I, thank God, met my obligations,
Not according to your merits,
But to my own qualifications,
I desperately need a vacation.

XXXIV

You seek to break off our affair,
Alas, this avowal, no doubt sincere
Overwhelms me with despair,
Be unfaithful, please my dear,
And continue to see me,
If not, at least, abuse me.

Endnotes

N ENDLESS LIST OF BOOKS AND ESSAYS HAS BEEN written over the years championing different points of view on the Portuguese letters. The most important works in France advocating Guilleragues as the author of Mariana's letters come from Frédéric Deloffre and Jacques Rougeot. Their book *Lettres Portugaises Valentins et autres oeuvres de Guilleragues*, published in 1962 by Classiques Garnier, is the basis from which further research was conducted and is the main reason behind the school of thought that the letters are a work of fiction. These two authors published subsequent books and essays on the letters, but I have limited my quotes to the 1962 edition. In Portugal, the book by Antonio Belard

Da Fonseca, *Mariana Alcoforado, a Freira de Beja e as "Lettres Portugaises,"* published in 1966, refutes Rougeot and Deloffre's theory (except when it comes to the writing style of the letters). Extremely well documented, it summarizes all the information known on Mariana; however, the book was never translated into French or English and did not have the impact it deserved.

The most complete studies on Mariana's life are found in four Portuguese books in particular. Luciano Cordeiro's book, *Soror Mariana, A Freira Portugesa,* published in 1888, was the first serious study to establish Mariana's existence. Manuel Ribeiro published his *Vida e Morte de Madre Mariana Alcoforado* in 1940 to celebrate the 300th anniversary of her birth, followed by Antonio Da Fonseca's book and more recently, in 1994, Alfredo Saramago published a wonderfully detailed book on the daily practices of the nuns called *Convento de Soror Mariana Alcoforado, Real Mosteiro de Nossa Senhora da Concieção.* None of these books has been translated into English or French.

Much of the information on Chamilly's life as a young man was found in Eugene Beauvois's *La jeunesse du Maréchal de Chamilly. Notice sur Noël Bouton & sa Famille de 1636 à 1667* (published in 1885) and *Les trois chamilly pendant et après la guerre de dévolution 1667–1671* (1886).

I found the details of Portuguese life in the works of British, French, and Portuguese historians.

English works include: John Colbatch (1664–1748), the diaries of Samuel Pepys (1633–1703), and Edgar Prestage

(1869–1951). Letters and papers from Sir Robert Southwell (an ambassador to Portugal from 1667–1668) were found at the British Museum. French works include Frémont d'Ablancourt's first-hand account of Schomberg's time in Portugal, that was essential in establishing the whereabouts of Chamilly during his time in Beja (1666–1667). Also from l'Abbé Vertot's (1655 1735) *History of the revolution of Portugal* (1689) and in General Dumouriez's (1739–1823) detailed description of Schomberg's Portuguese battles. Original documents concerning Barbin's Royal privileges are available at the Bibliothèque Nationale de Paris and at the Minuterie Centrale. Many original documents concerning details of everyday life in Portugal during the seventeenth century, royal decrees, descriptions of Dom Afonso's and Dom Pedro's weddings, the Queen Regent's funeral, and religious life were found at Lisbon's National Library.

I discovered many interesting details on this time period and some of the people in this book but as they were peripheral to the story I thought it best to include them in a general note section. I cite a source specifically only when I quote directly from an author.

PROLOGUE

1. (p. xviii) The spelling of Alcoforada with an *a* at the end is correct. The Portuguese language uses the ending *a* to indicate the feminine and *o* for the masculine. Over the years the tendency has been to refer to Mariana's last name in the masculine form to facilitate comprehension for non-Portuguese speakers.

2. (p. xix) Journal de l'Empire, 5 January 1810, quoted in Claude Aveline's book *Tout le rest n'est rien*. Mercure de France, Paris, 1951.

3. (p. xix) Deloffre, Frédéric, *Lettres*. Classique Garmier: Paris, des Saints-Pères, 1962 p. 1.

CHAPTER 1

1. (p. 2) Territories occupied by Portugal at the height of its empire during the fifteenth and sixteenth centuries included the islands of Madeira, Terceira, Saint-Michael, Prince, and Saint-Thomas, the islands of Cape Verde and of Saint-Laurence—the southern and western coasts of Africa—the kingdoms of Sofala, Mozambique, and Melinda. The Portuguese built the fort of western Ethiopia and established themselves in the kingdoms of the Congo and Angola. They passed the Red Sea, traveled the Persian Gulf, entered India, and dominated the isle of Ormus and the isle of Goa. Chaul, Caman, Bazaim, Cananor, and all of the Malabar Coast was theirs, including the Island of Ceilans. They occupied Malacca beyond the Gangue and won over the Persians, the Turks, the Arabs, the Moors, Bengali, Aracan, Pegu, and Siam. They built the town of Macao in China and they were the first to trade with Japan. They owned Brazil, Tangiers, and Bombay (now Mumbai).

2. (p. 2) John Colbatch in his history *An Account of the Court of Portugal under the Reign of King Dom Pedro* writes "Night-Walkers of all Ranks and Orders, from those of the first Quality, down to the very Fryars . . . A Dozen, or more Fryars would sally in Night upon Adventures . . . the Portuguese saying among the People was, 'That is equally dangerous to deal with a Fryar by Night, as with a Fidalgo by Day.'" (p. 11)

3. (p. 3) December 1, 1640, seven conspirators, together with twenty young men hidden in liveries, made their way to the palace. Entering the Spanish representative's room, they threatened the keeper of the door who, to save his life, nodded toward a hidden armoire. Cowering under stacks of papers was the most reviled man in

the country. Each of the men struck him once and threw the body out of the palace window to a populace hungry for blood. The enemy surrendered without resisting and John VI of Braganza would be proclaimed king before the end of the year.

4. (p. 3) The Romans founded Beja, formerly known as Pax Julia, on the highest point in the lower Alentejo. Four hundred years of Moorish occupation followed and many of the customs were integrated within the population's way of life, though the town was recaptured from the Moors in 1162. Today, it is still surrounded by immense plains that lose themselves into the horizon.

5. (p. 4) Unlike French society, where women enjoyed relative freedom, Portuguese women were constant victims of violence. Aggressions committed by men against women must have been frequent because King John IV created a law in 1652, subjecting men who hit women in the face or battered them to an investigation analogous to homicide.

6. (p. 4) A woman could not pass next to a man's hand because she would get pinched in a manner that would take half an arm or a full calf and would leave the poor unfortunate limping for half an hour—while the perpetrator boasted of his exploits to his friends. (*Bulletin des Études Portugaises* p. 22)

7. (p. 4) Ironically, despite men's treatment of women, Portugal was recognized throughout Europe as the country of love. Platonic love was considered the highest form of love. For the poet Tomé Pinheiro da Veiga, for example, the only true love is that which is content with little—"the gift of a letter, the favor of a gentle gaze, the suavity of a white hand." He adds, "It is the appetite that renders food appetizing, it is thirst that gives flavor to water." This may be the reason why nuns were so loved. (*Bulletin des Études Portugaises,* p. 25)

8. (p. 6) A religious military order which largely financed and inspired Portugal's explorations.

9. (p. 9) Concieção means conception. The convent is one of the finest examples of the Manuelina style of architecture. The convent connected to Dom Fernando's palace by a passage that led to the upper choir. A kind of pulpit or window opened onto the chapel

and it is believed that Dom Fernando's wife spoke to the population from there.

10. (p. 14) Catherine of Braganza, the daughter of the Queen Regent, left to marry Charles II of England on May 31, 1662. Despite being extremely close to her mother, historians noted that Catherine showed no emotion.

11. (p. 15) Throughout religious history, nuns like Saint Teresa were only awarded power within the larger Church community if they heard voices or received visions from God. Saint Teresa invoked fits of trembling (now believed to be epilepsy) in order to be heard by church officials.

12. (p. 17) Al Sousa Gomes in his *Madre Mariana Alcoforado, sua graca e su amor* (Lisbon, 1964) discovered an 1808 catalogue regarding the publication of a *Dictionary of Anonymous Works* by A. Barbier published in 1874. There is a note next to the entry regarding the Portuguese letters that claims the author as a Madame Pédégache. Sousa believes this Pédégache was a French nun living under the name of Madre Maria Leonor de S. Luis who taught French during the time Mariana was at the convent. He surmises she helped Mariana translate or translated Mariana's letters, which would explain Pédégache's name in the catalogue. Not much credence has been given to the possibility of Pédégache's translating the letters but Pédégache's presence at the convent presupposes that French was being taught.

CHAPTER 2

1. (p. 21) Dom Afonso and Dom Pedro were not being groomed for the mantle of king, and they would have been discouraged from learning to read or write in order to prevent them from having aspirations to the throne. This was common practice. Louis XIV's brother, whom everyone called Monsieur, was raised wearing dresses by his mother for the very purpose of keeping him away from the Crown.

2. (p. 22) The Treaty of the Pyrenees (1659) signed between Spain and France was negotiated by Cardinal Mazarin (the lover of Louis XIV's mother, Queen Anne of Austria, who was Spanish

by birth), and stopped France from getting involved with the Portuguese war. However, the French general Turenne feared that peace would give Spain time to recover and enable her to attack France a second time, draining France once again of its men and its resources. Secret meetings took place between Turenne and the Portuguese Ambassador, the Conde de Soure. Turenne hid him in one of his homes and Schomberg was entreated to lead the Portuguese army without Mazarin's knowledge.

3. (p. 23) Mazarin's spies informed him of Turenne's plans and he and Louis' mother tried to dissuade Schomberg from going. The queen tugged at Turenne's sleeve one day after having warned Schomberg not to go to Portugal: "Know you not, Monsieur de Turenne, that I see beyond Spain all the way into Portugal. But I am not worried for I have got what I wanted." (The queen meant she had obtained peace between Spain and France.) Schomberg's departure to Portugal was fraught with difficulties. Tipped off by Mazarin, the Spanish pursued Schomberg, forcing him to change ships midway, and hide aboard an English frigate.

4. (p. 28) Until the reign of Louis XIV, French nobility (including Chamilly's father, Nicholas Bouton) trained in Holland under Maurice de Nassau, commander in chief of the Netherlands and military strategist of note. Nassau reinvented the art of war. Resurrecting Roman war strategies, Nassau created mobile and flexible battalions that were disciplined, light, and well trained. He devised a technique by which soldiers formed three to six ranks, the first to shoot, the second readying to shoot, and the third to recharge. This enabled foot soldiers to break a cavalry charge. Nassau also developed a new system of defense by extending the protective boundaries of cities through the use of trenches filled with water. Until Nassau, armies were a composite of men intent on pillaging, looting, and raping. Turenne and Chamilly's father were trained by Nassau, who taught them that generosity, selflessness, and courage made better soldiers. Chamilly embodied all these virtues and was considered the new kind of soldier.

5. (p. 29) Herard married Catherine Lecomte de Nonant, the daughter of a wealthy merchant, in 1662. Mariana refers to Chamilly's sister-in-law in her second letter.

6. (p. 31) The population of Lisbon was between 165,000 and 200,000 and was comparable to Venice or Amsterdam, important cities at the time.

7. (p. 32) The reputation of British soldiers was such that the mere sighting of the blue and red wool caps they wore sent the enemy running in the opposite direction. The Castle Rodrigo situated in the south of the Alentejo, whose importance was in its location, held two hundred and fifty soldiers. Eight thousand Spaniards and nine cannons were sent to take it. Schomberg set out to rescue the castle. The regional commander, Pedro Jacques de Magalians, was nine miles away. Quickly assembling four thousand foot soldiers and six hundred horses, he began marching at night. En route, Magalians's men took the area's traditional blue and red capes worn by the peasant women and made bonnets for themselves. By morning the Portuguese soldiers had taken position between the Castle and the assailants. The Spanish were so frightened at the sight of the bonnets that they fled screaming. "The British are coming, the British are coming." Pursued by the Portuguese soldiers still wearing the made-up bonnets, the Spanish left all the baggage behind as well as their cannons. Seventeen hundred prisoners were taken. Only twenty Portuguese soldiers died and six were wounded.

8. (p. 32) To understand Chamilly's title of captain, here is the nomenclature of the French army.

An infantry squadron called a battalion by the French consisted of approximately 500 men.

One battalion usually consisted of four companies of 125 men each.

Three battalions (1500 soldiers) formed a regiment.

A regiment was commanded by a colonel.

A battalion was commanded by a lieutenant colonel.

A company was commanded by a captain.

A field master was second in command and almost invariably a nobleman, who usually exercised direct command over the aristocratic cavalry.

The word "baggage" means the army's portable equipment.

9. (p. 37) The window of Mertola, as it is still called today, stood taller than most men and was large enough to accommodate several onlookers. From it you could step onto a terrace that served as balcony, from where you could see the fields in the direction of Mertola and beyond toward Spain. The city of Mertola, fifty-four kilometers away and separated from Beja by a mountain ridge, could not be seen from that vantage, but the window overlooked one of the seven portals that Dom Afonso III had carved in the ancient Roman wall that surrounded the city. Each portal carried the name of the nearest town it looked toward, hence the name given to the window. This window was 50 paces away from the Mertola gate, hence its name. It has often been cited as proof the letters are fictitious because Mariana says she saw Chamilly pass on "that balcony from where we can see Mertola." She may quite simply have been referring to the portal. Furthermore the definition of a balcony as stated in gazette of the period, the "Mercure Français," (1663) volume IX explains that a balcony is "a sort of window that extends outward" which is accurate when describing the window of Mertola as it jutted out onto a terrace forming a balcony of sorts.

10. (p. 38) Dom Afonso ordered that plays of an impious nature be performed in convents.

11. (p. 40) The Portuguese infantry was poorly equipped, using the clumsy matchlock that weighed between fifteen and twenty-five pounds, and was fired from a forked rest. The powder was ignited by a slow match that forced the pike men to protect the gunmen while they advanced, repositioned themselves, and reloaded. The Spanish cavalrymen were armed with the lighter, handier flintlock that weighed only eleven pounds. Fired from the shoulder, it was easier to load, with a rate of fire doubled to one round per minute.

12. (p. 42) Schomberg's command and calm during the battle was best illustrated when a great discharge of cannon fire sent hundreds of men and horses crashing down a mountainside. He exclaimed to the officer next to him, "Do you not think that this resembles those ancient battle scenes, in which the world believes the painter's fancy has had the greatest share?"

CHAPTER 3

1. (p. 43) The French sat down in Paris with the Portuguese ambassador on February 27, 1666, to ratify the contract between King Dom Afonso VI and Marie-Françoise-Isabelle de Savorie, duchess of Aumale, known as Mademoiselle de Nemours. The marquis de Sande had crossed the channel incognito to sign the agreement and was violently ill on the way. He shaved his mustache and wore a wig as disguise. The king's mother died that same night.

2. (p. 45) French scholars Rougeot and Deloffre go to great lengths to establish literary parallels between Mariana's description of the first time she sees Chamilly and ancient poets:

"I imagined that when you halted you were quite happy to allow me to see you better so that I may admire your skill and good graces when riding horse. A sense of fright took me by surprise when you made it pass a difficult tract." Mariana letter 2

Compared to:

"If you curb the neck of a proud horse, I admire how you make it twirl in a tight circle." Ovide, Héroïdes, IV *Lettres Portugaises Valentins et autres oeuvres* p. 9)

or again in Letter 1 Mariana writes

"I stopped myself from returning to a life that must end, since I cannot keep it for you; at last, despite myself, I saw light. I flattered myself thinking I was dying of love; moreover I was relieved to no longer witness my heart being ripped apart by the pain of your absence."

Compared to:

"I resent them for not having allowed an unfortunate soul to die. When the feelings came back, so did the hurt." Ovide, Héroïdes, XIII (p.10)

Rougeot and Deloffre argue that Guilleragues found his inspiration in other writers and that he modified only the way in which he expressed feelings. However, the feelings expressed in Mariana's letters belong to the realm of human experience. Consequently, they can be equated to a wealth of writings, novels, poems, and true-life events.

3. (p. 46) Recognizing the benefits of color-coded clothing, Schomberg decided that the French and the Germans should wear gray and blue jackets with different colored linings in each. The concept of the French uniform was born and would remain greatly unchanged until the first World War.

4. (p. 46) A few theories exist on how Chamilly was introduced to Mariana. Chamilly first met the Portuguese commander-in-chief, Gil Vaz de Lobo, at the debacle of Cabeça de Vide. His sister, Madre Cecilia Sebastiana da Silveira, who was soon to be elected abbess at Mariana's convent, may have introduced the French soldiers to the convent, Chamilly among them. Rui de Melo, Mariana's brother-in-law, recognized as a ferocious fighter, would also have wanted to introduce the soldiers to the convent's inhabitants.

5. (p. 48) Frenchmen's interest in cooking is well documented. The seventeenth century was no exception. The marquise de Sablé's biographer, Victor Cousin, takes evident pleasure in quoting missives from La Rochefoucauld, Saint-Pol's father, who would constantly ask the marquise de Sablé for her roast beef recipes, jam recipes, and all manners of dishes.

6. (p. 53) Contrary weather detained the convoy longer than anticipated and the new queen finally left on July fourth, a week after she had wed. She embarked on a French warship under the command of the marquis de Ruvigni. Her fleet was comprised of two battleships, eight merchant ships, and another eight small crafts that attached themselves to the convoy in the hope of escaping pirates. A heavy fog settled shortly after their departure, the ships were separated, and the voyage took thirty-two days. The Queen finally arrived on August 2, 1666.

7. (p. 54) The Abbé of Saint Romain, France's secret envoy to the court of Lisbon, said of Dom Afonso, "He was a figure very strange to see. His fatness was due to his eating habits. He was an

enormous eater, devouring rather than eating. He drank heavily at his meals and in great gulps, and often became stupid and sleepy in consequence, in spite of the two glasses of water he took afterwards. He was often sick after his meals, probably due to the fact that he took most of his meals in bed." Dom Afonso smoked constantly and always carried a charge of snuff up his nose. He indulged in promiscuous sex and had a passion for bull fights. "As a result of this unhealthy life style Afonso is said to have suffered from offensive skin disorders, which made him take a bath twice a day" (D'Auvergne, *Bride of Two Kings*, p. 114). Dom Afonso's cleanliness must have appeared extremely strange to Marie-Françoise. The French bathed only once a month because the Catholic church viewed the use of soap as sinful and considered bathing a lustful activity.

8. (p. 55) Versailles was in the process of being built and the king traveled from castle to castle, staying in one place until the smell of urine became unbearable and then he would move to another castle.

9. (p. 55) Marie-Françoise was initially promised to Dom Pedro until her older sister rejected Dom Afonso in favor of an Italian prince. One must wonder what Marie-Françoise's thoughts were when she finally met the two brothers.

10. (p. 59) The gargoyles depicting crouching nuns in the birth position are less surprising once you know that the convent had an orphanage and that historians believe that children of nuns and priests were often raised there.

11. (p. 60) The only archival document ever to be found referring to Chamilly is a royal decree where it is said that the count of Saint-Léger had lost seventeen horses in the battle of Cabeça de Vide, signed October 18, 1667.

CHAPTER 4

1. (p. 74) This was not the first complaint. In June 1667 the authorities of Beja received an answer to the complaint which they had made of "the oppression which the French cavalry continued

to exercise on these people." (Edgar Prestage, preface to his translation of 1897, p. 13) The danger of scandal was even greater considering that Miguel was close to Dom Pedro, who gave him gifts of
jewelry. Miguel's dislike of the French presence may have been fueled by doubts he might have had concerning the friendship between Mariana and Chamilly.

2. (p. 82) Briquemault knew Herard as a fellow Burgundian
but also because Herard was elected to be responsible for the affairs
of the nobles and Briquemault would have had dealings with him.

3. (p. 84) Detractors have often cited that Chamilly's use of the
southern route was improbable, quoting that the soldiers normally
departed from Lisbon. But at the time Chamilly was trying to leave,
Lisbon was not a practical choice. Furthermore, the Marine Museum
of Lisbon has in its possession documents proving the southern
route to France a popular route often used by Frenchmen. Chamilly
would have easily found a passage to Marseille through the Algarve.
By using the southern route, Chamilly cut his voyage by 500 km (over
300 miles), which represented three days of travel time by horse.

Detractors also argue that the Algarve had long belonged to Portugal when Mariana wrote her letters. However, it has since been
proven that the expression *the Kingdom of the Algarve* was the popular
way of referring to the region during this time period and would remain so for quite a few generations.

It is interesting to note that French soldiers remained ready for
combat and on Portuguese soil until June 1668 while war records
place Chamilly in Dijon at his brother's castle on the ninth of February 1668. It's likely Chamilly left Portugal in December 1667 or in
the early days of 1668. No other documents have been found granting French officers of Chamilly's rank permission to leave Portugal
before the war was over.

The attack on Franche-Comté cannot be considered the cause for
Chamilly's departure, only the excuse. Chamilly was not enlisted
when he arrived in Dijon and he joined the attack as a volunteer. The
regiment promised to him in the document was not ready, and two
months would pass before it was organized.

THE LETTERS

1. (p. 89) In Barbin's edition from this point on, Mariana passes from the familiar "tu" (you) in French, to the more formal "vous" (thou). The Portuguese language did not use the "thou" and it is most likely that Guilleragues or Barbin decided to use the "thou" going forward. Portuguese translators simply restore the letters to the "you," but French scholars who believe the letters were written by Guilleragues debate whether if in the first sentence, Mariana is admonishing love—the concept—or Chamilly the lover.

2. (p. 97) Those in favor of the letters being a work of fiction use this supposed geographical mistake to make their case. The sentence is easily explained if one accepts that Mariana referred to the Mertola gate or portal, fifty paces away.

3. (p. 109) Two little Portuguese lackeys (note from Barbin's original edition). The Portuguese scholar Manuel Ribeiro discovered that Balthazar subsequently hired a servant Manoel, he believes used to be the one who worked for Chamilly.

4. (p. 115) Only Mariana's father was alive at this point but Mariana uses the Portuguese meaning that includes family members.

CHAPTER 5

1. (p. 119) The historian Cordeiro thought Chamilly may have left from Setubal, a port nearer Lisbon, which would indicate Chamilly tried to board in Lisbon before realizing French ships were not leaving.

2. (p. 122) Eleonord Bouton—younger brother of Chamilly. Eleonord was responsible for a priory of Artois in Franche-Comté when his brothers attacked. In keeping with the Chamilly spirit of loyalty and adventure, he helped win the war for France by convincing the town aldermen to surrender. Unfortunately Franche-Comté returned to Spain following the treaty of Aix-la-Chapelle. Peasants, angry at the role Eleonord had played in the battle, surrounded his priory and broke down the doors, forcing Eleonord to hide in the

church vault. He escaped at night pursued by the villagers screaming, "Judas, kill Judas." Barely reaching the cemetery wall,
Eleonord jumped, falling to the river below. Swimming in total
darkness, he made his way to a neighboring town and from there
to Herard's castle in Dijon.

3. (p. 122) Pierre Paillot, the renowned genealogist, was busy
compiling data at the time Chamilly was at his brother's castle, yet
Chamilly's stay in Portugal is barely mentioned. Historians intent
on glorifying Chamilly's exploits rarely mention Portugal despite
the importance of the war. Similarly, few Portuguese documents
mention Chamilly. Many Portuguese scholars surmise that a cover-
up may have taken place to protect the Alcoforado reputation and
eliminate any knowledge of the affair.

4. (p. 127) In *The Age of Conversation*, Benedetta Craveri gives a
wonderfully detailed overview of the salons (seventeenth century until the eighteenth century) and offers a comprehensive bibliography
of the works she consulted for her research.

5. (p. 128) The king himself had no privacy. No difference was
made between private and public life. Every room in Versailles, except for the king's bedchamber, was accessible to the public. Even in
his bedchamber, the king was never alone. Dozens of aristocrats
and ministers witnessed his rising every morning. Louis XIV's even-
tual downfall was in part due to the fact that his most secret war
plans were easily accessible. Secret letters that had passed between
Herard and Condé masterminding the taking of Franche-Comté
were published only two years after the attack. Louis' ministers wrote
in code to try and circumvent the problem but to no avail. The king's
correspondence was seldom if ever private. His letters were always
accompanied by secret instructions. However, even the secret instructions did not stay secret very long.

6. (p. 130) A few years prior to the events of this story, the marquise shared a house with one of her best friends, the countess de
Maure. To avoid catching a cold, the marquise had resorted to conversing through a folding screen. Small notes were handed back and
forth through servants, covering subjects as diverse as the weather,

health, plans for the day, a recipe, or a simple thought. Letters had never been used for this purpose before and the short missives rapidly gained in popularity. Soon all of Paris adopted what is today known as the "memo."

7. (p. 135) This story comes from *La médaille curieuse où sont gravés les deux principaux éceuils de tous les jeunes coeurs, Nouvelle manière de roman.* (The strange medal where is engraved the two main pitfalls of all young hearts new kind of novel.) L.C.D.V. Paris, 1672—found in A. Adam's *History of French Literature in the XVII century,* volume IV p. 182.

8. (p. 138) Henriette d'Angleterre commissioned the famous playwright Racine to write *Bérénice.* She is also known for asking two playwrights to each write a play on the same subject without informing either that the other had been asked.

9. (p. 138) Viala states that around 1660, one needed approximately 3000 pounds a year (roughly $11,550 U.S.) to be socially acceptable. A successful writer had the same standard of living as tutors, secretaries, bailiffs, making slightly more than schoolteachers and historians. A middle-rung writer is compared to a specialized laborer and a less successful writer to a coachman or a lackey.

10. (p. 139) A registered privilege gave a publisher exclusive rights to the material for five years. This law served to protect authors from fraudulent publishers.

11. (p. 142) The order created by Barbin is often compared to the five perfect acts of a tragedy. Books and essays exist claiming the letters are perfectly positioned even though they make no chronological sense.

12. (p. 144) The letters were so popular that within two years they had already become proverbial. Mme. de Sevigné (one of the most famous French letter writers of her century), writing in a letter dated July 19, 1671, to her daughter Mme. de Grignan:

> "Brancas has written me a letter so excessively tender . . . if I answered him in the same manner, I would be writing a 'portugaise.'" Again to the Count de Guitaut: "She has written in that tone all the 'Portugaises' in the world."

Under the care of the Great Condé's brother, the prince of Conti, Guilleragues' immediate needs were taken care of, but when at the death of his patron, he lost the financial support, it became imperative for Guilleragues to find himself a new benefactor. He would have known that getting published would help him immensely in securing a position. The valentines were circulating as early as 1667, two years before Mariana's letters. His circumstances suggest that had he been capable of being published before 1669, he would have. He had not even written enough valentines to publish them on their own, therefore Barbin had to supplement the book by adding a few random letters written by Guilleragues (that did not even speak of love), including one addressed to the marquise de Sablé, which was probably there to trade on the popularity of her name. Also included were some *Questions d'amour* (Questions of Love) that had already been published in another book. These Questions of Love were by Roger Bussy Rabutin, Chamilly's old commander. I have often wondered if Barbin, who loved to play games, chose Bussy-Rabutin because of his connection to Chamilly.

Because the value of old currency is sometimes difficult to assess, it is best exemplified by establishing some comparables. French cents are referred to as cents and French pounds are referred to as pounds.

What things cost in France circa 1669:

A meal in a bad inn (bread, meat, beer)	5 cents
A pair of clogs	4 cents
A small house (1 chimney, 2 doors, 2 windows)	200 pounds
1 lb sugar	14 pounds
1 lb meat	5 cents
1 pint of wine	4 cents
Upkeep of a horse	22 cents per day
1½ lbs of bread	3 cents

What a Frenchman earned:

A wine laborer	12 cents a day
A soldier	5 cents a day (plus 2 lbs of bread, 1 lb of meat, plus 1 pint of wine during military outings)
A sergeant	10 cents a day
A colonel	6,000 pounds a year
A priest working for an important household	200 pounds a year on top of which room and board plus amenities such as a horse were included. This could mean between 600 and 1000 pounds a year, in an urban setting.
A lackey working for an important household	100 pounds a year
A coachman working for an important household	100 pounds a year

Alain Viala, in his book, *La naissance de l'écrivain (The Birth of the Writer)*, says that Molière made 2000 pounds a year, enough to provide him with a comfortable apartment and one or two servants. This salary allowed him to live on an equal footing with a middle-class merchant or a nobleman of modest means.

CHAPTER 6

1. (p. 146) The law required he provide a detailed account of his lands and though he was already years late, Chamilly would eventually comply in 1685. The list, finished on March 10, 1670, was not submitted until 1685 according to Eugene Beauvois, in *Les Trois Chamilly,* page 439.

2. (p. 154) In his book, *The Great Generals of France*, Dussieux writes in a footnote on page 169: "It is in Portugal that he had the adventures we owe the Portuguese letters to, that gave M. de Chamilly such a great reputation among his contemporaries."

CHAPTER 7

1. (p. 155) *Lettres Portugaises traduites en François* (Amsterdam: chez Isaac Van Dyck, 1669).

2. (p. 155) *Lettres d'amour d'une religieuse escrites au Chevalier de C. Officier François en Portugal* (Cologne: chez Pierre du Marteau, 1669).

3. (p. 156) Counterfeit editions were not so subtle and Chamilly and Guilleragues are explicitly mentioned, though even in those prefaces, the publisher adds a clue to identify the exact Chamilly brother. In Alain Niderst's erudite and entertaining book, *Guilleragues, Subligny et Challe: Des Lettres Portugaises aux Illustres Françaises* (Saint-Genouph: Nizet, 1999), Chamilly is referred to as a "Cavalier," a clever clue signifying the second born, subtly indicating which of the Chamilly brothers the letters referred to.

4. (p. 156) Preface translated by Lisa Forrell for the 1992 production at the Etcetera Theatre, in London.

5. (p. 157) Bury, Emmanuel, *Lettres Portugaises*, Libraire Générale française, Paris, 2003, citing Jean-Michel Pelous' *Amour précieux, amour gallant (1654–1675): essai sur la représentation de l'amour dans la littérature et la société mondaine* (Paris: Librairie Klincksieck, 1980).

6. (p. 157) Cousin, Victor, *Madame de Sablé: Études sur les femmes illustres et la société de XVII siècle* (Paris: Didier, 1854).

7. (p. 158) ibid.

8. (p. 159) Guéret, Gabriel, *La promenade de Saint-Cloud*, Monval G. editor, p. 35–37 Nouvelle Collection Molièresque, n. XVI, Paris, 1888.

9. (p. 159) The book was first published in 1689 and was extremely successful. The first publication did not include the letters.

10. (p. 159) Chupeau, Jacques, "Les remaniements des Lettres Portugaises dans le Recueil des plus belles Lettres Françaises de

Pierre Richelet. Etude de Style," *Le Français Moderne* (January 1970): 57.

11. (p. 160) Rousseau, Jean-Jacques, "Letter on the arts to d'Alambert," 1748.

12. (p. 161) Green, Frederick C., "Who was the Author of the 'Lettres Portugaises,'" *The Modern Language Review* (April 1926): 162. Manuscripts from the seventeenth century after spell Guilleragues with a "q" instead of a "g".

13. (p. 161) ibid., concluding remarks of Green's paper (see p. 167).

14. (p. 161) Craveri, Benedetta, *L'âge de la conversation* (Paris: Gallimard, 2002), credits Guilleragues as the author, based on the findings of Rougeot and Deloffre; see p. 133.

15. (p. 162) Adam, A., *Histoire de la littérature Française au XVII siècle*, 2nd ed., p. 170, as cited in Emmanuel Bury, p. 10 (see endnote 6, above).

16. (p. 162) Coulet, Henri, *Les Lettres Portugaises et le roman épistolaire*, p. 225, as cited in Emmanuel Bury, p. 24.

17. (p. 162) The original line "Philarque a bonne mine, l'esprit vif, et est fort agréeable en compagnie. Il a beaucoup d'érudition, il fait très bien les vers, aussi bien que les lettres amoureuses." ("Philarque has good appearance, a nimble mind, and is great company. He is very learned, he does rhymes very well, just like love letters.")

18. (p. 163) Chupeau, Jacques, "Vanel et l'énigme des 'Lettres Portugaises,'" *Revue d'histoire littéraire de la France* (March–April 1968): 224.

19. (p. 163) ibid., p. 227.

20. (p. 164) Bury, Emmanuel, *Lettres d'une religieuse Portugaise* (Paris: Librairie Générale Française, 2003), p. 15.

21. (p. 164) Deloffre and Rougeot, p. 32.

22. (p. 165) Viala, Alain, *Naissance de l'écrivain: sociologie de la littérature à l'âge classique* (Paris: Minuit, 1985), pp. 119; 128.

23. (p. 165) ibid., p. 125.

24. (p. 167) Lassalle, Thérèse and Jean-Pierre, "Papers on French Seventeenth Century Literature," *Biblio 17* (1982). The Lassalles,

who discovered the manuscript, conclude that Guilleragues must have written *both* sets of letters.

25. (p. 167) Lafuma, Louis, *"L'auteur présumé du discours sur les passions de l'amour,"* Delmas, Paris, 1950, p. 16.

26. (p. 168) Carrell, Susan Lee, *Le Soliloque de la passion féminine ou le dialogue illusoire: étude d'une formule monophonique de la littérature épistolaire* (Tübingen: Gunter Narr Verlag), 1982.

27. (p. 168) Chupeau, Jacques, "Vanel et l'énigme des 'Lettres Portugaises,'" (*Revue d'histoire littéraire de la France,* March–April 1968).

28. (p. 169) Zabus, Chantal, *The African Palimpsest: Indigenization of Language in the West African Europhone Novel* (Amsterdam: Rodopi), 1991.

29. (p. 169) Leclerc, Catherine, "Des langues en partage? Cohabitation du français et de l'anglais en littérature contemporaine" (Ph.D. dissertation, Humanities program, Concordia University, Montréal, Québec, 2004).

30. (p. 170) D'Ablancourt, Frémont, Jean-Jacob, "Mémoires de Monsieur d'Ablancourt, envoyé de sa majesté Très-Chrétienne, Louis XIV en Portugal . . ." (La Haye: chez Jacob Van Ellinckhuysen, 1701).

31. (p. 170) Des Roches, "Journal Véritable de ce qui s'est passé en Candie sous Monsieur le Duc de la Feuillade," (Paris: Charles Serci, 1670).

32. (p. 170) Aristocratic French women were expected to speak Italian.

33. (p. 171) The fado is still extremely popular today.

34. (p. 172) Deloffre, F. et Rougeot, J. *Lettres portugaises, Valentins et autres oeuvres de Guilleragues.* Paris: Editions Garnier Frères, 6, rues des Saint-Pères, 1962. p. LXXXV.

35. (p. 172) Ibid p. LXXXVI.

Selected Bibliography

Alcoforado, Mariana. *Lettres portugaises traduites en français*. Preface and notes by Emmanuel Bury. Paris: Librairie Générale Française, 2003.

Alcoforado, Mariana. *Lettres portugaises et suites*, Preface and notes by Anne-Marie Clin-Lalande. Paris: le livre de poche, la Flèche Librairie générale française, Imprimeur Brodard et Taupin, 1993.

Alcoforado, Mariana. *The Portuguese Letters*. Translated by Donald E. Ericson. New York: Crown Publishers, 1941.

Alcoforado, Mariana. *Lettres de la religieuse portugaise, suivies d'une étude historique & de notes par Louise Delapierre*. Vol. 25, *Classique*. Paris: Club Français du Livre, 1951.

Alcoforado, Mariana. *Letters from a Portuguese Nun*. Translated by Raymond Mortimer. London: Hamish Hamilton, 1956.

Alcoforado, Mariana. *The Letters of a Portuguese Nun*. Translated by Edgar Prestage. London: David Nutt in the Strand, 1893.

Alcoforado, Mariana. *The Letters of a Portuguese Nun*. Translated by Edgar Prestage. London: David Nutt in the Strand, 1897.

Alcoforado, Mariana. *Lettres d'amour d'une religieuse portugaise à un officier français 1667–1668*. Preface and notes by Colonel Albert de Rochas. Grenoble: Imprimerie Allier Frères, 1908.

Allent, Pierre Alexandre Joseph. *Histoire du corps impérial du génie*. Paris: Magimel, 1805.

André, Louis. *Louis XIV et l'Europe*. Paris: Editions Albin Michel, 1950.

Arenal, Electa. "The Convent as Catalyst for Autonomy: Two Hispanic Nuns of the Seventeenth Century." In *Women in Hispanic Literature: Icons and Fallen Idols*, edited by Beth Miller. Berkeley: University of California Press, 1983.

Asse, Eugène. *Lettres Portugaises de Marianna Alcoforado avec les réponses*. Genève: Slatkine Reprints, 1970.

Aveline, Claude. *Et tout le reste n'est rien, la religieuse portugaise avec le texte de ses lettres*. Paris: Mercure de France, 1986.

Barrett-Browning, Elizabeth. *Sonnets from the Portuguese: Illuminated by the Brownings' Love Letters*. Edited by Julia Markus and William S. Peterson. Hopewell, N.J.: Ecco Press, 1996.

Basto, Arthur de Magalhaes. "La vie et les moeurs de la société portugaise au XVIIe siècle (Conference Transcript)." *Bulletin des études portugaises* (February 1940): 20–42.

Bathélémy, Edouard de. *Les amis de la marquise de Sablé*. Paris: Dentu, 1865.

Beauvois, Eugène. *Les trois Chamilly pendant et après la guerre de dévolution*. Beaune: Imprimerie Arthur Batault, 1886.

Beauvois, Eugène. *La Jeunesse du Maréchal de Chamilly, notice sur Noël Bouton et sa famille de 1636 a 1667*. Beaune: Imprimerie Arthur Batault, 1885.

Béguillet, Edmé and Courtépée, Claude. *Description générale et particuière du duché de Bourgogne*, 3rd ed. Avallon: Editions F.E.R.N.; Paris: Guénégaud, 1967–1968.

Beirão, Caetano. *A Short History of Portugal*. Translated by Frank Holiday. Lisbon: Edicões Panorama, 1960.

Besset, Auguste. *Un illustre bourguignon, Noël Bouton, Marquis de Chamilly, Maréchal de France 1636–1715*. Macon: Protat Frères, Imprimeurs, 1909.

Birmingham, David. *A Concise History of Portugal*. 2nd ed. Cambridge: Cambridge University Press, 2003.

Boileau, Nicholas Despreaux. *Epistre à monsieur de Guilleragues*. Paris: Denys Thierry Saint-Jacques, 1674.

Bordeaux, Henry. *Marianna la religieuse portugaise*. Paris: Albin Michel, 22 rue Huyghens, 1934.

Bouchot, Auguste. *Histoire du Portugal et de ses colonies*. Paris: Librairie Hachette et cie, 1854.

Bouton, Jean de la Croix. "Le Maréchal de Chamilly et le contexte historique des lettres portugaises." *Annales de Bourgogne* 34 (April–June 1962).

Bray, Bernard, Landy-Houillon Isabelle. *Lettres portuguaises, lettres d'une péruvienne et autres romans d 'amour par lettre.* Paris: Flammarion, 1983.

Brito, Castro e. *A Docaria De Beja Na Tradicao Provincial.* Lisboa: Editorial Imperio, I.D.A, 1940.

Bussy, Roger de Rabutin, comte de. *Histoire amoureuse des Gaules.* chronology and preface by Antoine Adam. Paris: Garnier-Flammarion, 1967.

Caetano Pereira e Sousa, Joaquim Jose. "Classes de Crimes." Lisboa, 1803.

Cardim, Luis. "Les lettres portugaises." *Bulletin des études portugaises* (1931): 161–73.

Carrell, Susan Lee. *Le soliloque de la passion féminine ou le dialogue illusoire.* Tubingen; Paris: Gunter Narr Verlag; Editions Jean-Michel Place, 1982.

Castro, Júlio de Melo de. *Historia Panegyrica Da Vida De Dinis De Mello De Castro.* Lisboa: Off. de António Duarte Pimenta, 1995.

Chéruel, Adolphe. *Mémoires de Mlle de Montpensier.* Paris: Charpentier, 1858.

Chupeau, Jacques. "La lettre amoureuse au XVIIe siècle, des fleurs du bien dire au language du coeur (Transcript of Symposium Held at the University of François-Rabelais, Tours Sept. 18–19, 1998)." *Epistolaire Antique* (2000).

Chupeau, Jacques. "La mobilité sociale au XVIIe siècle." In *XVIIe siècle avec le concours du centre national des lettres* (January–March 1979).

Chupeau, Jacques. "Les remaniements des lettres portugaises dans le recueil des plus belles lettres françaises de Pierre Richelet. Étude de style." In *Le Français moderne* (January 1970).

Chupeau, Jacques. "A propos de quelques éditions oubliées des lettres portugaises." In *Revue d'histoire littéraire de la France* (January–February 1972).

Chupeau, Jacques. "Remarques sur la genèse des 'Lettres portugaises'." In *Revue d'histoire littéraire de la France* (May–August 1969).

Chupeau, Jacques. "Vanel et l'énigme des 'Lettres portugaises'." In *Revue d'histoire littéraire de la France* (March–April 1968).

Coelho, Jacinto do Prado. *Dicionario De Literatura*. Vol. 2: Figueirinhas, 1997.

Colbatch, John. *An Account of the Court of Portugal, under the Reign of the Present King, Dom Pedro II*. London: Printed for Thomas Bennet, 1700.

Constant, Jean-Marie. *La vie quotidienne de la noblesse française aux XVIe et XVIIe siècle*. Paris: Hachette Litterature, 1985.

Cordeiro, Luciano. *Sóror Mariana, a Freira Portuguesa*. 2nd ed. Lisboa: Livraria Ferin, 1888.

Cornette, Joël. *Le roi de guerre: essai sur la souveraineté dans la France du grand siècle*. Paris: Payot, 1993.

Cosnac, Daniel. *Mémoires de Daniel de Cosnac*. Tomes I et II. Paris: Chez Jules Renouard et Cie libraire de la société de l'histoire de France, 1852.

Cousin, Victor. *Mme. de Sablé: Études sur les femmes illustres et la société du XVIIe siècle*. Paris: Didier, 1854.

Craveri, Benedetta. *Láge de la conversation*, Éliane Deschamps-Pria, translator. Paris: Gallimard, 2002.

D'Ablancourt, Frémont Jean-Jacob. *Mémoires de Monsieur d'Ablancourt, Envoyé de sa majesté très-chrétienne, Louis XIV en Portugal*. La Haye: Chez Jacob Van Ellinckhuysen, 1701.

D'Ablancourt, Jean-Jacob. *Memoirs of the Sieur D'Ablancourt*. London: Ralph Smith and James Round, 1703.

Dangeau, Phillippe de Courcillon, marquis de. *Journal du marquis de Dageneau publié en entier pour la première fois par MM. Soulié, Dussieux, de Chennevières, Mantz, de Montaiglon, avec les additions inédites du duc de Saint-Simon publiées par M. Feuillet de Conches*. Paris: Firmin Didot frères, 1854–1860.

D'Auvergne, Edmund B. *The Bride of Two Kings: A Forgotten Tragedy of the Portuguese Court*. New York: D. Appleton and Co., 1911.

De Sourches, Marquis. *Mémoires du marquis de Sourches sous le règne de Louis XIV*. Tome premier, publiés par le comte de Cosnac. Paris: Librairie Hachette et Cie, 1882.

Dédéyan, Charles. *Madame de Lafayette*. Paris: Société d'enseignement supérieur, 1965.

Delavigne, Marcelle Faucher. *Visite à la religieuse portugaise*. Paris: La Palatine, 1961.

Delgado, Manuel Joaquim. *Ensaio Monografico (Historico, Biografico, Linguistico E Critico) Acerca De Beja E Dos Bejenses Mais Ilustres*. Beja: Camara Municipal de Beja, 1973.

Deloffre, Frédéric. Rougeot, Jacques. *Lettres portugaises, Valentins et autres oeuvres de Guilleragues*. Paris: Editions Garnier Frères, 6, rue des Saints-Pères, 1962.

Deloffre, Frédéric. "Madame de la Sablière et ses Familiers." In *Vie des salons et activités littéraires: de Marguerite de Valois à Mme de Staël: actes du colloque international de Nancy*, edited by Roger Marchal. (6–8 Octobre 1999).

Deloffre, Frédéric, and Jacques Rougeot. *Correspondance*. Tome 1 et 2, Textes littéraires français, Genèva; Paris: Droz, 1976.

Denis, Ferdinand. *Portugal*. Paris: Firmin Didot frères, 1846.

Des-Roches. *Journal véritable de ce qui s'est passé en Candie sous monsieur le duc de La Feuillade*. Paris: Charles de Sercy, 1670.

Des Jardins, Marie-Hortense, Mlle. *Receuil de quelques lettres ou relations galantes*. Paris: Claude Barbin, 1668.

Des Vasconcelos, Jose Cerqueira. *As Cartas Da Religiosa Portuguesa, Nunes De Carvalho*. Lisboa, 1935.

Donneau de Vizé, Jean. *L'amour échapé, Ou les diverses manières d'aymer*. Paris: Thomas Iolly, November 12, 1669.

Dumouriez, Charles François Du Perier. *Campagnes du maréchal de Schomberg en Portugal, depuis L'année 1662 Jusqu'en 1668*. London: Cox, Sons, and Baylis, etc., 1807.

Dupuy, R. Ernest and Trevor N. *The Encyclopedia of Military History from 3500 B.C. To the Present*. 2nd revised ed. New York: Harper-Collins, 1986.

Durao, Paulo. "Compendios De Literatura Portuguesa—as Cartas Da Freira." In *Broteria* 16 (1933): 160–88.

Dussieux, Louis. *Les grands géneraux de Louis XIV, notices historiques*. Paris: Librairie Victor Lecoffre, 1888.

Ericeira, Francisco Xavier de Menezes, Conde da. "Historia De Portugal Restaurado." In *Biblioteca Histórica—Série Régia*, 134–313. Lisboa: Livraria Civilização, 1945–1946.

Ericeira, Francisco Xavier de Menezes, Conde da. *Relaclam da Campanha de Alemtejo no outono de 1712*. Lisboa: Na Officina de Miguel Manescal, 1714.

Fonseca, António Belard de. *Mariana Alcoforado: A Freira De Beja E as "Lettres portugaises"*. Lisboa: The Portugal–Brazil Press, 1966.

Formont, Maxime. "La religieuse portugaise." *Extr. de la Revue hebdomadaire* (October 14, 1893): 271–300.

Frederick II, King of Prussia. *Frederick the Great on the Art of War*. Translated by Jay Luvaas. Edited by Jay Luvaas. New York: The Free Press, 1966.

Frei, Charlotte. *Übersetzung als Fiktion, Die Rezeption der Lettres Portugaises durch Rainer Maria Rilke*. Germany: Peter Lang, 2004.

Fuller, J. F. C. (John Frederick Charles). *A Military History of the Western World: From the Defeat of the Spanish Armada to the Battle of Waterloo*. Vol. II. New York: Da Capo Press, 1987.

Gheyn, Jacob. *Maniement d'armes d'arquebuses, mousquets & picques*. Zutphen, 1619.

Gomes, A. Sousa. *Madre Mariana Alcoforado, Sua Graca E Seu Amor*. Lisboa, 1964.

Gourville, Jean Hérault de. *Mémoires de Gourville, publiés pour la société de l'histoire de France, par Léon Lecestre*. Paris: Paris, Librairie Renouard, H. Laurens, successeur, 1894–1895.

Green, F. C. "Who Was the Author of the Lettres Portugaises?" *The Modern Language Review* (1926): 159–67.

Grimberg, Carl. *Des guerres de religion au siècle de Louis XIV. trad. Gérard Colson; adaptation française sous la direction de Georges-H. Dumont*. Paris: Marabout, c. 1983.

Haag, Eugène and Émile. *La France protestante*. Vol. 9. Paris: Sandoz et Fischbacher, 1877–1888.

Harline, Craig. *The Burdens of Sister Margaret*. New York: Doubleday, 1994.

Henriot, Emile. *Les Livres du Second Rayon, irréguliers et libertins*. Paris: le Livre, Emile Chamontin, directeur, 1926.

Henriot, Emiles. *Livres et portraits (Courrier littéraire) Troisième série.* Paris: Les Petits-fils de Plon et Nourrit, 1927.

Ivanoff, Nicola. *La marquise de Sablé et son salon.* Paris: Les Presses Modernes, 1927.

Klobucka, Anna. *The Portuguese Nun: Formation of a National Myth.* Lewisburg: Bucknell University Press, 2000.

Krajewska, Barbara. *Mythes et découvertes: la salon littéraire de Madame de Rambouillet dans les lettres des contemporains.* Paris; Seattle: Papers on French Seventeenth Century Literature, 1990.

La Fuma, Louis. *L'auteur présumé du discours sur les passions de l'amour.* Paris: Delmas, 1950.

Labourdette, Jean-François. *La nation française à Lisbonne de 1669 à 1790.* Collection du centre d'études Portugaises 2. Paris: Fondation Calouste Gulbenkian, Centre culturel portugais, 1988.

Lacape, Henri. *La France et la restauration de Portugal.* Paris: Maurice Lavergne, Imprimeur 289, Rue Saint-Jacques, 1939.

Laclos, Choderlos de,Pierre. *Les Liaisons Dangereuses.* Paris: édition de René Pomeau. GF-Flammarion, 1996.

La Fontaine, Jean de la. *Les Amours de Psyché et de Cupidon.* Paris: Le livre de poche, Classique, 1991.

Lamy, Bernard. *La rhétorique ou l'art de parler.* Paris: Honoré Champion éditeur, 1998.

Lassalle, Jean-Pierre, Lassalle, Thérèse. *Un manuscrit des lettres d'une religieuse portugaise: leçons, interrogations, hypothèses.* Paris-Seattle-Tuebingen: Biblio 17-6, Papers on French Seventeenth Century Literature, 1982.

Leclerc, Catherine. "Des langues en partage? Cohabitation du français et de l'anglais en littérature contemporaine." Ph.D. diss. Presented for Humanities' program, Concordia University, 2004.

Maigret. "Enregistrements des privilèges commencant au mois d'octobre 1673." Bibliothèque Nationale de France, 1673.

Marques, A. H. de Oliveira. *Histoire du Portugal des origines à nos jours.* (translated from the Portuguese by Marie-Hélène Baudrillart), Saint-Etienne: Horvath, 1978.

Martins, Rocha. *Soror Mariana.* Vol. 2, *Os Grandes Amores De Portugal.* Lisboa: Coleccao Historia Rua Do Alecrim, 611. (n.d.)

Masson, Philippe. *Histoire de l'armée française*. Paris: Perrin, 1999.

Michel, Roland Francisque. *Les portugais en France, un français en Portugal*. Paris: Guillard, Aillaud & Cie, 1882.

Mignet, M. Francois Auguste-Marie, Alexis. *Négociations relatives à la succession d'Espagne sous Louis XIV*. Paris: Imprimerie Royale, 1835.

Moreri, Louis. *Le grand dictionnaire historique*. Edited by Étienne François Drouet. Paris: les libraires associés, 1759.

Niderst, Alain. *Essai d'histoire littéraire: Guilleragues, Subligny et Challe: Des "Lettres Portugaises" aux "Illustres Françaises"*. Saint-Genouph: Nizet, 1999.

Paillot, Pierre. *Historique généalogique de la maison de Bouton, au duché de Bourgogne*. Dijon: chez l'autheur, etc., 1665.

Paillot, Pierre. *Historique généalogique des comtes de Chamilly de la maison de Bouton, au duché de Bourgogne*. Dijon: chez l'autheur, etc., 1671.

Payne, Stanley G. *A History of Spain and Portugal*. Madison: University of Wisconsin Press, 1973.

Pelous, Jean Michel. *Amour précieux, amour galant: 1654–1675: essai sur la représentation de l'amour dans la littérature et la société mondaine*. Paris: Klincksieck, 1980.

Pepys, Samuel. *The Portugal History: or, A relation of the troubles that happened in the court of Portugal. In which is to be seen that great transaction of the renunciation of the crown by Alphonso the Sixth, the dissolution of his marriage with the Princess Maria Frances Isabella of Savoy: the marriage of the same princess to the Prince Don Pedro regent of the realm of Portugal, and the reasons alledged at Rome for the dispensation thereof*. London: Printed for Richard Tonson, 1677.

Piedagnel, Alexandre. *Lettres portugaises*. Paris: Librairie des Bibliophiles, 1876.

Pinard, M. *Chronologie historique-militaire–Table des rois de France, les secrétaires d'état à la guerre, les sénéchaux, les connétables et les commandants d'armées*. Vol. 1. Paris: C. Hérissart, 1760.

Pinard, M. *Chronologie historique-militaire–les lieutenants généraux des armées du Roi du 25 juillet 1762 et les maréchaux de camp jusqu'en 1715*. Vol. 6. Paris: C. Hérissart, 1763.

Prestage, Edgar. *The Diplomatic Relations of Portugal with France, England, and Holland from 1640 to 1668*. Watford: Voss and Michael, LTD, 1925.

Quincy, Charles Sevin, marquis de. *Histoire du règne de Louis le Grand, roy de France* . . . Paris: D. Mariette, 1726.

Ranft, Patricia. *Women and the Religious Life in Premodern Europe*. New York: St. Martin's Press, 1996.

Rattazzi, Marie Leizia Bonaparte-Wyse, Mme de Solms. *Le Portugal à vol d'oiseau*. Paris: A. Degorce-Cadot, 1883.

Reclam, Pierre-Christian-Frédéric and Erman, Jean-Pierre. *Mémoires pour servir à l'histoire des réfugiés français dans les états du roi de Prusse*. Berlin: J. Jaspard, 1782–1794.

Reed, Gervais. *Claude Barbin, Libraire à Paris*. Genève: Librairie Droz, 1974.

Ribeiro, Manuel. *Vida E Morte De Madre Mariana Alcoforado*. Lisboa: Libraria Sa da Costa, 1940.

Richardson, Samuel. *Clarissa, or the History of a Young Lady*. Edited by Angus Ross. Harmondsworth, Middlesex, England; New York City: Penguin Books, 1985.

Rilke, Rainier Maria. (translation of the *Lettres portugaises* by) *Portugiesische briefe, die briefe der Marianna Alcoforado*. Leipzig: Insel-Verlag, 1913.

Rohou, Jean. *Jean Racine entre sa carrière, son oeuvre et son dieu*. Paris: Fayard, 1992.

Rohou, Jean. *Lettres d'amour du XVIIe siècle, Marie-Catherine Desjardins, Lettres et billets gallants, Edme Boursault, Lettres de Babet, Guilleragues, Lettres portugaises*. Paris: Seuil, 1994.

Rodrigues, António Gonçalves. *Mariana Alcoforado, História E Crítica De Uma Fraude Literária*. Coimbra, 1935.

Roy, Jules. *Turenne: Sa vie, les institutions militaires de son temps*. Paris: A. Le Vasseur et cie, 1896.

Ruppert, Jacques. *Le Costume III*. Paris: Flammarion, 1931.

Sabugosa, Conde de. *Gente D'Algo*. Lisboa: Ferreira, 1915.

Saint-Simon, Louis de Rouvroy duc de. *Mémoires, Tome 41, Les grands ecrivains de la France*. Paris: Hachette, 1878–1928.

Saint-Simon, Louis de Rouvroy duc de. *Mémoires: additions au journal de Dangeau.* Paris: Gallimard, 1983.

Saramago, Alfredo. *Convento De Soror Mariana Alcoforado, Real Mosteiro De Nossa Senhora Da Conceição: Ensaio Histórico.* Sintra, Portugal: Colares Editora, 1994.

Scudéri, Madeleine de. *De l'air galant et autres conversations.* Paris: Honoré Champion editeur, 1998.

Serpa, C. J. *Enciclopedia Diocesana, Etudo Historico, Geografico, Etnologico, Religioso Da Diocese De Beja.* Beja, 1961.

Sousa, António Caetano de. *Justificada Com Instrumentos, E Escritores De Inviolavel Fé, E Offerecida a Elrey D. João V.* Lisboa: José Antonio da Silva, 1716.

Sousa, António Caetano de. *Provas Da Historia Genealogica Da Casa Real Portugueza.* Lisboa: Regia Officina Silviana, 1766.

Twiss, Richard. *Travels Through Portugal and Spain in 1772 and 1773.* London: Printed for the author, and sold by G. Robinson, T. Becket, and J. Robson, 1775.

Vertot, abbé de. *Histoire des révolutions de Portugal: Stéréotype d'Herman.* Paris: Mme Dabo-Butschert, 1825.

Viala, Alain. *Naissance de l'écrivain.* Paris: Les Editions de Minuit, 1985.

Visconti, Primi. *Mémoires sur la cour de Louis XIV, traduits de l'Italien par Jean Lemoine.* Paris: Calmant-Levi, 1908.

Weygand, Général Maxime. *Turenne, Les grands coeurs.* Paris: Flamarion, 1929.

Xavier, Angela Barreto. Cardim, Pedro. Alvarez, Fernando Bouza. *Festa Que Se Fizeram Pelo Casamento Do Rei D. Alfonso V I.* Lisboa: Quetzal Editores, 1996.

Zabus, Chantal. *The African Palimpsest: Indigenization Of Language In The West African Europhone Novel.* Amsterdam; Atlanta, GA: Rodopi, 1991.

Acknowledgments

Heartfelt thanks to my editor, JillEllyn Riley, whose perceptive notes, structural ideas, and enthusiasm deftly guided me through the last stages of the book. Her friendship is a precious gift. To my friend Steve Hutensky and to Jonathan Burnham, thank you for taking a chance on an untried author. Besides my husband, Caroline Alexander was the first to spur me on. I can never be thankful enough for her counsel, her encouragements, and sage advice that came at every juncture. I owe her more than I can say. This book could never have been written without the assistance of Prune Iris Catteau, who traveled from Paris to Lisbon in search of documents, Carolyn Chiasson-Cyr, who did the same in Montreal, and Maria Salmon for her help in translating the more difficult passages in Portuguese. My thanks to Laurie Nardone, who taught me to frame a question, to Susan Hatch, who was relentless in asking important questions, and to the scholars Catherine Leclerc, Jacques Chupeau, and Gervais Reed, for making their research available to me. Their findings were instrumental in elucidating my thoughts. My love and thanks to my sisters Christine and Isabelle, who are always there to encourage and support. I don't know what I would do without you. To Elizabeth Conway West, Michelle Ducroux, Ruth S. West, Robert Whalen, Shauna Baird, Leslie Lyman, Laura Apgar, Mary

Ellen De Biase, Eve Battaglia, Amy Povich, Sean Haberley, Cathy Anastas, and Cynthia Carlone, many thanks for reading the manuscript at various stages and to Katherine Vaz for her book on Mariana and introducing me to portraits of Mariana done by Matisse, Modigliani, and Braque. Thank you to my friends Maryam d'Abo, Christopher Hampton, Ele and Ben Shaw, Katherine McCubrey, Francois Ducroux, James Cripps, Barbara Spiridigliozzi, and Hamilton Fish for their support. Thank you to my lawyers Peter Grant and Larry Shire, my acting manager John DoHority, and my acting agent Steve Stone. To Kirthana Ramisetti for her work on the bibliography. To the Miramax team, who are so great at what they do: Robert Weisbach, Judy Hottensen, Catherine Finch, Noah Levy, Adrian Palacios, and the amazing Kristin Powers, thank you all for championing this book and making it your own. I could never have found time to write without the help of the wonderful Marelene Benz who takes care of my children, Laetitia (who was barely three when this all started, and Gabriel and then Jemma who were born during the process) with such love and devotion. She has all my gratitude and love. I owe my thanks to all those who participated in the New York production. Richard Hsu (set design), Luca Mosca (costumes), Rick Martin (lighting), Nancy Allen (sound design), Erik Sniedze (stage manager), and everyone at the Culture Project. Thank you to the actor Liev Schreiber for his participation and finally, thanks go to Alan Bushman, founder of the Culture Project, who once said his faith in my capabilities and his love for the letters led him to build a theater. Were it not for his gentle and persistent nudging, I would never have undertaken to perform the letters in New York.

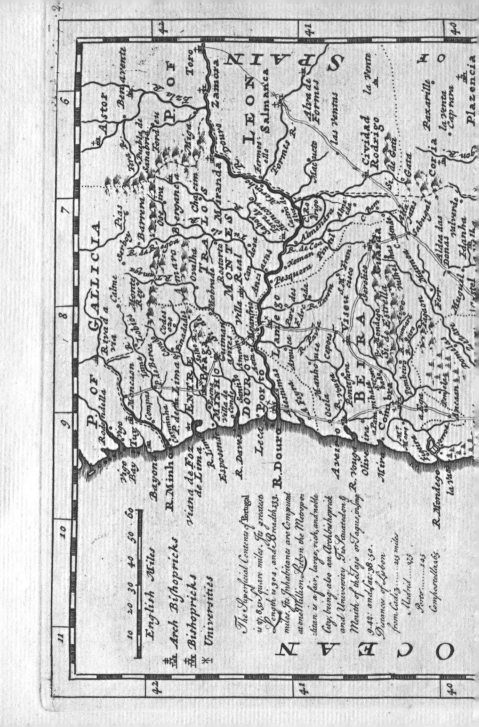